LEADERSHIP

Jim Selman

LEADERSHIP© BY JIM SELMAN

Direction: Cristina Shahinian

Special thanks to Annie Shahinian

Collaboration: Rocìo Rodriguez Etchard and Clarece
Distchekenian P. Vignoli

Our Acknowledgment to Gabriel Allen, Fernando Latorre and
Gustavo Valle for their testimonies.

ISBN: 1460953584
ISBN 13: 9781460953587

LEADERSHIP

Our Acknowledgment to Gabriel Allen,
Fernando Latorre and Gustavo Valle for
their testimonies.

TESTIMONY

FERNANDO J. LATORRE
Director of Corporate Banking Banco Itau Argentina

There are several reasons that motivate me to recommend Jim Selman's book. Without a doubt, the strongest reason is that I personally saw the transformation of work teams I formed part of in recent years, and achieved breakthrough results despite the general difficulties and unforeseen challenges of the market.

Without a doubt, this approach, as a starting point, came about in me through searching and studying about how to implement new methods or ways to motivate our people year after year and at the same time achieve high levels of results in our teams that are sustainable over time.

Facing our daily work problems while centering on our relationships and our language led to personal reflection and began to challenge all of its members to be more conscious of how we relate to one another, how we communicate, and how we commit ourselves to the company and our workplace. This sounds conceptually simple, and it goes together not just with being clear and establishing and defining the proposed objectives but with a process and repeated team practices that are necessary and useful to work on basic facts such as empathy, responsibility, and commitment. Basically, utilizing one of the exercises of "offering negative judgments," the team had some tense moments that helped to work out difficulties and personal differences in order to create more solid, transparent, and trusting relationships. From there on, establishing a shared vision was easier and more effective, where the impossible became possible and where a certain "reserve" of available potential was transformed into reality and concrete action.

In summary, Jim's book leads me to reflect on how, as leaders, we have the responsibility to always offer a positive outlook in order to propose to others that they give the best of themselves in performing the tasks that demand so much of them. Without a doubt, our optimism, together with our level of energy and conviction, converts—through conversations—this new possibility or ideal vision into reality and encourages people to change their reality, as difficult as it may be.

GABRIEL ALLEN
Vice President Brink's Latin America

Towards the end of 2001 and early 2002, a headhunter contacted me about forming part of a company evaluation project.

My lack of experience in this specific industry led me ask my future boss what he saw in me in order to offer me that position, as my previous work experience had nothing to do with this new line of business.

My future boss' answer was surprising: "We aren't looking for an industry expert, but rather a person capable of leading a transformational process in a company that is a world leader with its worst operation in an unpredictable country." (February 2002)

I made the commitment. I spent the first year setting up a team of people willing to carry out change in the organization and with others with backgrounds unrelated to the company but with skills in integration and teamwork.

It was a huge and complicated challenge given the organizational structure; it was very change-resistant, aggressively competitive, and within the context of an uncertain national outlook.

In October 2002, I had the opportunity to meet and work with Jim Selman and exchange opinions and points of view regarding the challenge I was facing. That was how I learned from ontological technology or discipline what *coaching-leadership* meant, the ability to create new futures; and I obtained a clear vision of what was needed to generate cultural change within the organization—to generate change in the level of communication, that is, to go from always doing the same thing to the concept of innovating, breaking our paradigms, getting rid of the idea that we can't do it or that there are no solutions, or that "we never did it that way" and instead look for a breakthrough result and go from being losers to being winners.

We all had to improve and be responsible for change; but the most important aspect was renewing our individual commitment to the vision and objectives to be achieved. Later, we positioned ourselves in the future, in how we would see our organization, and what we should do in order to achieve breakthrough results.

We had to change our organizational language, giving power to others and making them understand that they could achieve breakthrough results by acting together, not individually. The objective was to implement cultural change, positioning ourselves for the achievement of breakthrough results.

By communicating the passion of what we were doing, we achieved a commitment from each person in their own place and position as a member of a work team. In South America, our company has received more than we could have imagined, since in April 2010, only eight years after I accepted the challenge of leading it, Brinks Argentina was recognized as the best operation in the world.

GUSTAVO VALLE
President and Ceo Dannon US

I met Jim during my first assignment as general manager in 2003, one year after Argentina's big economic crisis. The business I was running, Aguas Danone de Argentina (Villavicencio and Villa de Sur, Danone's mineral water brands in Argentina), had just lost 25 percent of its revenues as well as the distribution of other beverages that had helped pay for distribution costs. The company went from having an acceptable level of earnings to losing money each month. The crisis led the management team to launch an ambitious plan for innovation, cost reduction, and the search for a more affordable alternative distribution plan.

The ideas were very good, and some of them changed the company's future, but the biggest challenge was changing team's mentalities and leading them to think about creating something totally new, forgetting all the difficulties of recent times, forgetting recent difficulties such as:

- We're in a crisis consumers have no money.
- We can't change the distribution we're working with the same people as always.
- We can't lower costs more than we already have; it was a huge effort.
- We already did this before and it didn't work," etc.

We worked with Jim so that the company's transformation would not only be a success but also a personal experience of growth and learning for everybody working in the company.

Unfortunately, I was with the company only for a short period of time, as the business grew so quickly that the group promoted me and I moved to Brazil to be the general manager of Danone Brazil. The situation in Brazil was similar, but it was an even greater challenge; the business was in bad shape, and the teams hadn't seen the light in years. Their self-confidence levels were extremely low.

In this case, the cycle lasted for five years and the results were even better. The transformation was so significant that not only is it still the largest and most dynamic company in the sector, but several of its managers today run even larger businesses.

On a personal level, it was a phenomenal process of transformation. Today I see management beyond the classic definition of organization, planning, control, and execution. I believe that the objective of a leader and a good manager is "coaching," making others see where they can go, beyond their own imagination.

What I learned from Jim during these years has allowed me to get to where I am and above all to imagine and build a future for myself that I would never have envisioned. *Transformation* best defines what I do. I continue to work with Jim in creating even bigger possibilities.

PROLOGUE

If we visit the Web site www.amazon.com, we will find that there are more than sixty-five thousand books that include the word *leader* or *leadership* in their title. While the number of books published is surprising, it is even more interesting if we ask ourselves why there are so many books written by so many people about this topic in particular.

Obviously, leadership is a topic that generates a great deal of interest. Nevertheless, we find that in these books there is no consensus about any aspect of the topic itself, what it is, and what one can learn about it.

Most of us can easily coincide that reading and understanding books about leadership does not produce leaders. The same is true of this book, but perhaps these articles can began to clarify the reason *why* reading and knowledge about leadership do not produce leaders.

circumstances, not a judgment of who is to blame for the circumstances. Responsibility is about ownership of the way things are; it is a state of being-in-the-world. No one can legislate responsibility or any other human quality—but responsibility can be learned and coached, and it can be the foundation for building a culture of leadership in which all of us share in creating the future.

From the point of view suggested in the CCMD course "Coaching for Breakthroughs and Commitment," responsibility is a declaration of "who one is" in a situation. The word literally means "response-ability": the freedom to act. When we take a stand, we bring ourselves forth as committed in a manner that is not subordinate to the circumstances or the conventional wisdom of what is and is not possible. For example, if we say "this is my country, my government, my organization, my circumstance, and my issue," then we might also say that "I am responsible" for everything in my environment—not as an admission of wrongdoing or having created the issue, but as a declaration that opens a possibility of choice and action.

If we aren't responsible individually, then there is no possibility beyond continuing to cope with circumstances that are bigger than we are, pray for better times, and do what we can to survive. Whatever the future, we can safely assume that it will be the product of action taken today…right now. This idea that the future is a product of action seems obvious whether we are speaking of making a date for coffee with a friend, planning an individual's career, or creating change in the public service. What is less obvious is that all of us are acting to the best of our ability based on the way we observe our circumstances, and our observations are a function of our historical stories of how the world works and what we believe to be possible. In other words, our actions are normally responses to our explanations and justifications for what has happened in the past. We assume that "the system" is more or less cast in stone, and therefore we normally commit only to what we think is reasonable and feasible. Actions based on this view, however, will always lead to more of the same based on the past and reinforce the cultural and circumstantial status quo. Perhaps this is what George Bernard Shaw had in mind when he said:

Reasonable people adapt themselves to the circumstances.

Unreasonable people adapt the circumstances to themselves.

Progress (leadership) depends upon unreasonable people.

What if we were committed to being unreasonable? What if we stopped blaming the system or the politicians or the media or our workloads for whatever we consider negative in our current situation? What if we transformed the idea of leadership from being a solution to a problem to being an expression of each individual's responsibility to create the future? What if our actions were based on our commitment to and responsibility for a future worth having...a vision of service through mutual respect, straight talk, full and open cooperation, and a culture in which we value individual differences?

To have these "what ifs" become "why nots" will require we take different actions than we might ordinarily take and challenge some of our most basic assumptions about the nature of our "reality." If we accept the premise that our actions are already correlated to the past, then it follows that to have a different future, we will require action that is a correlate of the future we are committed to creating. Our leaders need to stand for this possibility—not for reasonableness and not for excuses why it is hard to achieve our dreams in the current circumstances.

Becoming a leader and being responsible begins by accepting that whatever we consider to be real is always and only an interpretation. For example, in a recent speech, the clerk of the Privy Council challenged all of us to create a workplace that was more open to human values and creativity. This can be heard cynically as a reality in which he is merely cheerleading, or it can be heard as a reality in which he is calling for new forms of expression, new conversations about who we are, and new action consistent with what we say we want. The question isn't "what is reality?"; it is "what interpretation of reality are we committed to?"—and given that interpretation, "what actions are we taking?"

Another notion we should challenge is that one needs position, authority, or control to have power and to make a difference. In our history we have seen countless examples of individuals such as Mahatma Gandhi, Martin Luther King Junior, and Pierre Trudeau, or groups like Amnesty International and Greenpeace, taking a stand for what they considered to be right. While many might not agree with everything they espoused—and sometimes they had to pay a price, even their lives for what they stood for—they also shifted the larger conversations and interpretations for the rest of us and created a new reality based on a concern for the well-being of the whole society and future generations. These acts are always unreasonable; they always go against the prevailing wisdom and even sometimes against common sense.

Yet these are the most powerful acts of leadership imaginable; they are acts of individual human beings being responsible for their situations and moving forward from a deep sense of trust in their vision, other human beings, and a willingness to risk what is necessary to make a difference.

We can also challenge the idea that leaders are special people with some innate capacity that allows them to become leaders. A more powerful idea is that leaders are ordinary people who make extraordinary commitments. In addition, leadership doesn't happen inside an individual, but in the context of relationships and in the coordination of actions and practices in a community. In this sense it is a social phenomenon that is as much a product of those who follow as of those who are recognized and acknowledged as leaders.

In conclusion, we should constantly remind ourselves that the future doesn't happen "out there," and the future isn't a problem to be solved or a fixed reality waiting for us to arrive. The future is always a possibility, and when it arrives it will always be a function of our individual and collective actions... today.

Whether we are waiting for a great leader, aspiring to being leaders ourselves, or simply seeing leadership as missing in our current circumstances, our choice is whether we participate and are responsible for bringing leadership into existence or whether we wait and watch and assume that someone else is responsible. If we choose not to be responsible, then we are powerless and may end up with a future we do not want. On the other hand, if we can be responsible and participate in creating the future then as Mahatma Gandhi said, we are "being the change we wish to see." We are being responsible for leadership and working together to transform our difficult circumstances into the raw material with which to create a future worthy of who we are and what we stand for.

commitment is a universal phenomenon and basic to all human coordination. Commitment is the foundation for any kind of intentional change. If any company, organization, or nation is to have a future on the world stage, or any future beyond the predictable for that matter, it will be because its people are committed to that possibility and committed to actions to make it happen.

From my perspective, there are two kinds of change in our everyday experience of living: that which we make happen (such as starting a business, creating a new market, producing unprecedented results, or building a new product) and the kinds of change that seem to happen around us in the course of life itself (such as climate change, various "social" problems, and shifts in fashion). In the first instance, people are clearly committed to make something new happen. In the second instance, our choice is often to change ourselves in relationship to changes we did not conceive or intend—to cope with or adapt to a "new reality." In both instances, however, I suggest the key to accomplishment is our capacity to commit ourselves to creating something that did not exist for us previously—to invent new interpretations and practices for having our reality be consistent with our commitments. I meet few people who have a powerful distinction between commitment as the essential access to *creating or intentionally relating to change* and commitment as a kind of "lip service," a well-intended gesture.

A PARADOX

A paradox appears when we consider that the problem may be our common sense about change and commitment. On one hand, it can be argued that without commitment nothing will change, at least that we have anything to do with. We must accept whatever the circumstances of our lives give us and learn to cope effectively. This can lead to a kind of resignation and passive acceptance without real possibility of changing our world or ourselves. On the other hand, if we only commit to what our common sense tells us is feasible and possible, we will, by definition, have more of the same because common sense is our collective understanding of the world based on past experience and practices.

Yet anyone can identify dozens of examples of "realities" today that were unimaginable or made no sense only a few years ago and yet are becoming ordinary now. Consider the Internet, cell phones, cloning, fax machines, the collapse of the Soviet Union, expanding political awareness, terrorism, and the global economy as examples. Most of the people I meet in technological fields say they are working on solutions to problems that will be obsolete by the time they are implemented. At the current rate of knowledge expansion, we are rapidly approaching a time when almost anything we learn will be obsolete before we learn it. In such a world, to organize our thinking and our actions around what has worked in the past— our common sense—is a formula for ever-increasing anxiety and failure to achieve our ambitions.

I believe that some of the most pressing questions of our times relate to how to thrive and prosper in an increasingly unpredictable world. This discussion centers on questions about commitment. What is it? What does it mean to commit? How does our understanding of commitment shape our lives and possibilities? What are the consequences of making and keeping (or not keeping) commitments? What is our everyday relationship to commitments, our own and others? Most importantly, how can our commitments enhance our satisfaction in living, our effectiveness in accomplishing our ambitions, and our capacity to empower ourselves and other human beings?

LIVING AND WORKING IN A CONTEXT OF COMMITMENT

All human beings make commitments. Even the most ardent procrastinator will recognize at some point that he or she is committed to not making a decision. Sometimes we keep our commitments, and sometimes we don't. Commitment is a universal phenomenon. It has been argued that one of the things that distinguish human beings from the rest of the animal kingdom is that we have the capacity to generate and act consistent with our commitments (while the behavior of animals is a function of instinct). Without commitment, we could not coordinate actions. We would not have institutions such as marriage, enterprises could not exist, and even normal social interactions such as meeting someone for coffee would not occur. Life would be a random event. The future could never be more than a mechanistic extension of what has gone before, and life, for the most part, would be circumstantially determined.

The capacity to commit may be the most distinguishing and constitutive aspect of our existence as human beings. In spite of this, the term *commitment* and what it refers to is transparent for most of us most of the time. Most of us agree that commitment is important, but live as though it is a mere convention and that outcomes are a function of forces and factors outside ourselves. Moreover, most of us hold the idea of commitment in a sort of "moral" condition in which those who don't keep commitments are "bad" and those who do are "good." In this condition, we are essentially trained to only make those commitments that are virtually certain or very predictable based on past behavior. This condition is often reinforced by idle speculation, explanations, and justifications about what might happen if we fail to keep the commitment.

Explanations and justifications, however, are themselves projections of the past into the future. In my view, this perspective is a mistake and a pitfall that discourages taking risks, obscures responsibility for action and our relationship to commitment, and limits the possibility for creating positive change.

CHARACTERISTICS OF COMMITMENT

First and foremost, commitment is an action. To commit is to bring something into existence that wasn't there before. At the moment of its coming into existence, a commitment is a creative act, distinct from whatever reasons or rationale we might have for making the commitment. This action is being taken by and between human beings all the time. Whether we are committing to meeting a friend or paying a bill or going to school, we are always moving within a fabric of conscious and unconscious commitments. The action of committing is also always connected to the future—to another action, event, or result. When we commit, we are saying, "I will be responsible for something happening in the future which would not occur in the absence of my commitment." Commitment defines the relationship between a future that is entirely determined by historical circumstances and one that can be influenced, changed, or created by human beings. When we don't consciously commit or commit conditionally, we are in effect committed anyway—to the status quo.

A second important aspect of commitments is that they are not just personal. When we commit, we are also creating expectations on the part of others, and in some cases our commitments have a direct and important impact on the choices others have and how they perceive their future. Commitments have the characteristic of both opening particular futures and closing other futures simultaneously. When a parent commits to send a child to a private school, he or she is doing more than just providing an educational opportunity: the child is also being placed into a particular situation that will allow for choices or commitments which would not otherwise present themselves. Likewise, the commitments of our forefathers are passed to us as "reality," which we must either accept as our own or change by means of new commitments. In this sense, commitment is as much a social phenomenon as it is an expression of individual choices.

A third characteristic of commitment is that it exists only in our speaking and listening—in language. A commitment occurs in conversation as a "speech action," which brings into existence some desired future condition as a possibility that, when fulfilled, becomes a new "reality." The power of commitment is that it is the only action of which human beings are capable in which the future and the present appear in the same moment. When I promise to meet you, I am evoking the future time and circumstances of our meeting in the same moment as I speak the promise. In making the promise, I am committing to be at the meeting at the time and place we've agreed to. Likewise, if you requested the meeting or accept my offer, you've committed to be there also. In this sense, both promising and requesting are commitments to participate in creating particular futures together. If I am not serious about my promises and requests, you will stop listening to them as commitments and will not coordinate your actions with mine. The result will be chaotic, produce distrust or annoyance, and eventually we will either not communicate at all or, more likely (as is the common case), will implicitly agree to cope with whatever our circumstances allow and avoid the question of responsibility for our actions altogether.

THE POSSIBILITY OF CHANGE

Most of us live and work in environments that we say should change in one way or another. If we listen carefully to our own conversations and the conversations of others, we can notice that much of the time we are talking about our circumstances within the same perspective that we might use to observe a game or a movie. Our conversations are those of observers giving an account or telling a story about how we see or how we feel about our "reality." We can often hear people speaking about "the way we are in this country," the problems of the economy or the society or within a particular company, and why it is difficult to effect meaningful changes. What is transparent, however, is that these conversations rarely result in new commitments to action. In other words, our conversations about what needs to be done or what needs to change don't, in and of themselves, change anything! In fact, they reinforce the status quo and become self-fulfilling and self-justifying in nature. We live in a kind of "cultural drift" in which we must learn to cope with historically determined circumstances with very little power to effect change or create a future that is discontinuous with the past.

An everyday practical example of this can be seen when we speak with people in organizations and ask how much time is spent in meetings and how people evaluate the value of meetings. Predictably, we will hear there are too many meetings and most of them are a waste of time. At the same time, most people are complaining that they lack the time to do many of the things which they say need to be done. The conclusion most often reached is to have fewer meetings. This is, in turn, followed by all the reasons we can't really have fewer meetings or why we can't have our meetings be more productive. The general mood becomes one of "resignation" until we simply accept or put up with the status quo and go through the motions of meetings without concern for or expectation that they can ever change.

Unfortunately, most of the work human beings do—in fact most of our lives—happens in meetings with other people. Consider, for example, that a telephone or e-mail conversation is a kind of meeting, a sales call is a kind of meeting, and most planning occurs in meetings. Even social events or having a romantic dinner can be viewed as "meetings." Meetings are never a problem in and of themselves. We can all think of examples of meetings that were extraordinary, even life changing. What people are saying is that they spend too much time in meetings that are unproductive or unsatisfying. To a large extent, this is because people are speaking without commitment, or they lack competency in resolving differences and having effective dialogue. If we ask ourselves what we are committed to making happen in a meeting, and then organize our conversations around that commitment, we will begin to observe and experience a different meeting. Not only do we empower ourselves as actors in the meeting (as opposed to reacting to what is said), but we also begin to listen differently to what is occurring and have many options not normally apparent.

In the previous chapter, I quoted British writer George Bernard Shaw as having said, "Reasonable people adapt themselves to the circumstances. Unreasonable people adapt the circumstances to themselves. Progress depends on unreasonable people." I think it is appropriate to mention this quotation again here because it highlights the dilemma that confronts us when we seriously consider making fundamental changes in how we live, how we work, our business culture and our practices for coordination. It suggests that if we expect anything to change, we need to be *unreasonable*. More specifically, we need to make unreasonable commitments. If we only commit to what we think is reasonable or feasible, we are, by definition, making commitments to more of the same—to living in the cultural drift. "Reasons" are, by definition, products of past experience and common understandings for why things happen and what is or is not possible.

Being unreasonable is not the same as being unrealistic. Being unreasonable means acting in a manner that is inconsistent with conventional wisdom and common sense. Any example of significant change began with someone making a commitment to a possibility that was viewed as unreasonable or impossible at the time. Commitment is the difference between living in a context of responsibility for creating the future versus living in a context of reasonableness in which we must cope with whatever the circumstances give us.

CREATING A CONTEXT OF COMMITMENT

The question that arises now, of course, is how to shift our "way of being" from one of reasonableness and historical inertia to one of commitment and empowerment. One of the things I have learned in my work is that people place a great deal of value on intelligence and knowledge. In a world that doesn't change or that changes very slowly, this value makes sense and is even practical since there is time to learn and apply what we know. In a world that is changing at exponential rates, however, conventional intelligence and knowledge are often obsolete before we have time to apply them. If we need proof or established acceptance of knowledge before we act, then it is

To illustrate how this happens, I am reminded of a recent conference we conducted for an organization in Canada that was by everyone's account extraordinary. The leadership team of the company declared a new future for themselves, had breakthroughs in their relationships with one another, and generated powerful commitments to action. Near the end of the conference, I asked, "What will be the first question people will ask you when you return to the office?" The obvious response was, "What happened" or "How was the conference"? The normal response would have been, "Fine" or "Great" or a description of what actually happened. I asked, "What is the 'reality' of this meeting in the future? Is it what in fact happened or is it in the conversations you and other people will have *about* what happened?" The conference participants acknowledged that the future reality would be in the conversations about the meeting. They speculated that these conversations would probably be that the leaders went off to another meeting and that it was just another example of top people getting benefits and that the meeting didn't have much impact or effect on people's day-to-day experience. I then asked, "If the future reality was a function of what you say when asked the question, what could you say?" They acknowledged that they could declare the meeting to be a historical turning point, they could share their personal breakthroughs, and they could make new promises to people or begin to open new conversations for changing their relationships with those asking the questions. The result of having created new conversations in the company was that the value of the meeting went far beyond what actually occurred or the experience of the individual participants. The meeting was the occasion for the participants to exercise their leadership in shaping the perceptions of the people in their company and also in enrolling them in new possibilities for change in the future. By changing everyday conversations, they began to create a new culture based on commitment and possibility.

CULTURE AS BACKGROUND CONVERSATIONS

"Culture"—whether viewed from the perspective of an individual, an organization, or a society—does not exist as a factual "reality" independent of our background (transparent) conversations about:

- What is and is not possible
- What limits or constrains action
- Who we are
- How we deal with differences and contention, and
- Our relationship to learning and commitment.

This "cultural interpretation" forms the basis for how we listen and speak to one another, shapes our day-to-day practices, and ultimately determines how we see and relate to our "reality" (which, in turn, determines our behavior).

Creating a new cultural context requires creating new background conversations. Background conversations are obvious, so obvious, in fact, that we don't normally think about them, which is why they are in the background. If you live on a busy street, at some moment you stop noticing the noise and are even surprised when a visitor points it out to you. For example, what comes to mind when I ask, "What is it that everybody in your organization 'knows' about how to be successful here?" In a group situation, what will quickly emerge is a combination of:

- **Unspoken and often unexamined rules and assumptions.** For example, be careful, don't complain, don't make mistakes, don't park in the boss's parking spot, keep information to yourself, be sure you have a solution before you expose a problem, as unconscious behavior based on historical obligations—commitments made in the past—that come to us as tradition, background conversations, and unexamined practices always justified and reinforced by our interpretations of the world. Historically determined and unconscious behaviors are essentially automatic "re-actions," not authentic commitments in the present moment.

From the perspective of commitment as an action, we could conclude that the answer to creating change—to living a more productive and satisfying life and being more responsible—is captured in the Nike slogan, "Just do it." Most will agree, however, that knowing what to do and doing it are not the same. Cultures are constituted to persist. The nature of this persistence can be heard in the rationale or conversations we have about why we don't "just commit" and then do whatever it takes to fulfill our commitments. For some, it is "I don't know how," for others it may be fear of what others will think or do, and for others still it may be connected to distrust or past experiences that were unsatisfactory.

A more fundamental understanding of commitment is that it is directly related to our "way of being" in the world—what we stand for, our core values, and the integrity with which we lead our lives. Many people do their best, behave, and act in ways that are positive and intended to contribute. Few, however, consider that we also have a choice about "who we are." If we observe people's everyday behavior and conversations, we can see that there are many ways to answer: I am (name), I am my job, I am my family, I am my moods, I am my feelings, I am my appetites, I am my addictions, I am my money, etc.

We rarely hear people say, "I am my commitments" or "I am who and what I say I am." In part this is due to how we formulate and use the word *commitment* in everyday conversations. We often say, "I have a commitment" in the same context as we might say, "I have a cold." This subtle formulation in everyday language is another example of how we relate to commitment as something separate and apart from ourselves, rather than an expression of who we are in action and the possibility of a future other than that available from the inertia of the past.

I am not suggesting an "ultimate truth" here. I am saying the answer is always an interpretation we mostly inherit from our cultural practices, and that the interpretation we live will limit or open our possibilities and actions. When we are conscious of and responsible for the interpretation that defines our "way of being" in the world and can stand for a more powerful interpretation such as "I am my word," we have possibilities and choices that are beyond the ordinary. From this perspective, the future becomes a subject for action and design, rather than our having to simply cope with the generalized circumstances of life. In our work, we do not suggest that we can or need to teach people how to be committed. Nor is it necessary to endlessly debate what are the "right" commitments. If all commitments are conditional, then it becomes an academic discussion; and if we are responsible for our commitments and subsequently learn we were wrong, we always have the wherewithal to make new commitments to correct our mistakes.

We, as consultants, believe that commitment is a natural and constant aspect of life available to all human beings. It is necessary, however, for people to "unlearn" many of the unexamined concepts and assumptions about their worldview, commitment, and possibility for them to recognize this for themselves. Further, we find that when people are aware of this and are shown that they have a choice and that their commitments and their relationship to commitment make a difference, they begin to exercise the choice and begin to live as their word—to be responsible.

In most organizational cultures, our practices suggest that the answer to the "who are we" question is that people are objects that need to be controlled to perform the functions necessary to accomplish various tasks. Even our most basic notions of management, such as its responsibility for providing motivation, is built on this assumption. And yet, if we have learned anything in the past fifteen years of global competition, it is that we can no longer rely on a few leaders at the top of an organization to direct and control the work of everyone else. The whole concept of "empowerment" is based in the practical recognition that an enterprise cannot survive without everyone involved self-generating results based in their own intelligence and commitments.

Powerful competitors are those that are learning to "free the human spirit," to empower people to *be* responsible, to be committed, and to coordinate their commitments in the service of a vision worth working for.

> *Until one is committed there is hesitancy, the chance to draw back, always ineffectiveness. Concerning all acts of initiative (and creation), there is one elementary truth, the ignorance of which kills countless ideas and splendid plans: that the moment one definitely commits oneself, then Providence moves, too. All sorts of things occur to help one that would never otherwise have occurred. A whole stream of events issues from the decision, raising in one's favor all manner of unforeseen incidents*

and meeting and material assistance, which no man could have dreamt would have come his way.

I have learned a deep respect for one of Goethe's couplets: *"Whatever you can do, or dream you can, begin it."*

W.H.Murrey, the leader of the Scottish Expedition to Mt.Everest.

CHAPTER 3

INNOVATION

Innovation is one of those words that we all use, agree is a positive thing, and for the most part want more of. The term *innovation*, like the word *leadership*, however, seems to defy generally accepted understanding. Most of us lack a shared interpretation of what we mean or what we are observing when we use these terms. Moreover, we lack practices for deliberately and consistently producing whatever is meant or whatever it is that we are looking for from "leadership and innovation." This is evident in the fact that in spite of thousands of books on these subjects, reading and understanding the books doesn't enable us to be leaders or to be innovative. These terms are closely related. *Leadership* always has some focus on bringing about a desired future. We would not normally consider a spectator of the status quo to be a leader. The term *innovation* also suggests some break with the norm or status quo. I am suggesting that an innovator and a leader are cut from the same am claiming that our relationship to the circumstances, especially when there are breakdowns, is the primary factor in determining whether we respond as leaders and innovate or simply resist or cope with what is happening.

Whether we are speaking about leadership or innovation, our concern is almost always about accomplishing some sustainable change whether large or small. Change can occur gradually and in small increments such as making continuous improvement to an existing process or product. Change may also occur as a breakthrough such as some unprecedented action or result that opens possibilities for new occurrence. While leaders and innovators participate in both kinds of change, I distinguish leadership as always occurring in a context of some intention to create a breakthrough...to break with the status quo. A one-time, unique event is not an innovation. For an occurrence to be a breakthrough it must alter, change, illuminate, or modify the existing structure(s) within which the innovation is occurring. In other words, we might say that this kind of innovation is the kind of action or outcome that alters the context, paradigm, or frame of reference of the innovator and those who have a stake in the innovation. We conclude that innovation changes the innovator and the space of possibilities available for everyone. Leadership is about creating what does not exist—bringing forth something that was previously "not real" or not available within an historical context. Leadership isn't just about what happens within boundaries; it transforms our relationship with boundaries and circumstance.

As previously noted, change is happening all the time. To observe a change we must be comparing our perception of how things appear now with how we remember them from before; change is an assessment or an assertion that something is different than it was. The time frame for comparison may vary. For example, technology has changed the way we do our work compared to ten or fifteen years ago; it probably hasn't changed much in how we work today as compared to yesterday. By the same token, the resources we have to work with have undoubtedly changed from yesterday. At a molecular and biological level, our bodies are changing with each breath we take. If we wish to develop a rigorous methodology for deliberate and intentional innovation and leadership, we need begin with this question: "How do we relate to our circumstances and change?"

RELATIONSHIP TO CIRCUMSTANCE AND CHANGE

There are six different ways we can relate to our circumstance and the changes that are occurring all the time. The way we relate to our circumstances becomes the foundation for our being leaders and opens or closes possibilities and opportunities for innovating. If we consider that change is a constant and always occurring whether we know it or not, then we might also say these six ways of relating to the circumstances are also ways we relate to the world and become the contexts within which we deal with everyday life. These should not be considered as progressive steps in a process. Rather, these are different "states of being" or contexts available to every human being, at every moment, to differing degrees depending upon our commitments, concerns, and competence in various domains of action.

RESISTANCE—OPPOSITION TO CIRCUMSTANCE

Probably the most common way we relate to change is to resist it. To resist means to stand apart from whatever we are resisting and judge it as "not being as it should be."

We resist in many ways; we can resist by simply disagreeing with a new policy or by analyzing something over and over again, or by playing devil's advocate with no ownership of the issue. Resistance can be overt or covert; sometimes we can resist by agreeing with someone and then gossiping when the person isn't around. We can procrastinate, we can argue, we can rationalize or even sabotage a leadership initiative simply by ignoring it and waiting for the next change to come along.

Whatever strategies or patterns for resistance we have, whether overt or covert, whether conscious or unconscious, whether active or passive they have three things in common:

First, all forms of resistance are "counter-innovative" and thwart human intentionality to create change. Any effort spent in opposing what is occurring moment to moment will blind us to possibility. Further, resistance gives power to the status quo or cultural inertia which, by its nature, will persist. This is reflected in the often-quoted maxim "the more things change the more they say the same."

Secondly, all resistance is rooted in the past and is grounded in a negative mood/attitude and assessment of "the way it is"…a judgment that things "should be" different than they are. Our commitments and actions are organized by what we see as feasible and that we know how to do. At best, this will lead to finding effective ways to cope and at worst will lead to a state of chronic suffering and eventually to resignation.

Thirdly, to resist implies that there is something "there" to resist that essentially objectifies our world, including ourselves and other people, turning us into objects in an objective world. This reduces us to being victims of whatever it is we are resisting and/or encourages a "spectator" relationship with the circumstances. This means we no longer participate in creating the future, and become trapped in a worldview that destroys possibility and power. In this state, innovation is a rarity and an ideal. When innovation does happen it is usually attributed to some "special-ness" of the innovator or more often explained as an anomaly that leaves us unaffected, untouched, and not responsible for the change.

"Leadership" in this context will involve "opposition" to the circumstance and for the most part will prove ineffective to the point of becoming part of the problem. For example, in most organizational or cultural "change" initiatives, the prevailing rational is that the status quo is "broken" and needs to be fixed. The leadership is resisting the "way it is" and in a well-meaning way is attempting to "fix it." The problem is that these initiatives are rarely effective because everything being done to change something is pushing against (resisting) what is already going on. This is how many issues persist even when there is widespread agreement that something should change. Essentially the proponents and opponents of a leadership initiative are operating in the same context.

COPING—POSITIVE REACTION TO CIRCUMSTANCES

Coping is also rooted in a view that circumstances are objective and we must somehow adjust our commitments and actions to match what the circumstances allow. Coping might be viewed as a positive alternative to resistance in which one works within the circumstances effectively. Energy that was previously expended in resisting is redirected to problem solving and designing ways to overcome barriers to accomplishing one's intention. In this sense coping is also "counter-innovative" as a relationship to change; however, there is one big difference: specifically, there are many innovations that are conceived as tools or strategies for more effective coping. In other words, in a circumstantially determined view of reality, coping can drive innovation, but only as a *reaction* to the circumstances, not as an intentional force in creating new circumstances.

For example, "organized labor" was invented as a re-action to perceived misuse and abuse of power by owners and managers in the early part of the twentieth century and has become an integral aspect of how work is accomplished. In other words, the political-economic "institution" of organized labor was a way for workers to cope with their circumstances. While we can observe that this "innovation" has produced a lot of value and benefit for workers over the years, it can also be argued that it has done little to build or address the underlying issues of trust and allocation of perceived power in organizational hierarchies. In effect, the mechanism for coping has reinforced and even institutionalized the prob-lem. Further, we can argue that successful coping solutions will often thwart and even undermine attempts at further innovations. In the above example, labor organizations have generally attempted to block various proposed innovations in management such as cross-functional training, incentive compensation packages, self-managing teams, and commit-ment-based management.

Leadership in this context is often facilitative and oriented toward reasonable expectations and interpretations of what is possible and not possible. In a coping context, leaders will typi-cally be arguing for and justifying whatever limitations seem to exist, and encouraging "work around" or "in spite of" strategies for getting things done. While this can be positive and pro-duce results, the leader in this case becomes a well-meaning and unwitting coconspirator in individual and organizational limitations.

RESPONDING—OWNING THE CIRCUMSTANCES

To respond means to freely choose action, given the circumstances. To respond requires a different relationship to the circumstance in which we consider that the circumstances are subordinate to the actions of the individual. In other words, to respond requires that we view ourselves as responsible, as owning, as being senior to whatever circumstance is occurring. The word *responsibility* can actually be seen as "the ability to respond"..."response-ability."

In responding, we see human beings as having insights and making choices in relationship to objective circumstances but not limited or defined by them. When we are responding we are beginning to innovate to the extent that we:

a) have some intention or commitment.

b) are owning and not "re-acting" to circumstances.

c) are bringing something new into existence, which whether small or large has value/utility and can be sustained/replicated in the future.

For example, one of the most basic organizational issues is the common "us versus them" conversation. In this structure, we complain is that "they" are a problem. "They" might be upper management or the quality control group or the salespeople or the government. The underlying structure of the conversation is that someone "outside" is causing a problem for me/us.

To respond requires that we acknowledge that whoever "they" are is occurring within our interpretation of the world. Our choices and actions are never limited or determined by "them" or the circumstances unless we believe that we have no power or choice in the matter; what limits us is part of our interpretation. We are never, in fact, victims of our circumstances, although in many instances it can seem so, and our suffering when this is the case can be very "real."

Secondly, to respond we must grant "them" autonomy as individuals—the freedom to choose, the legitimacy of their view even if we disagree. Otherwise we will be reacting to what we perceive "they" are doing and therefore have limited action and become part of a larger pattern of resistance that reinforces "their" behavior. In a posture of resistance, at best we may "win" in a dispute by dominating rather than innovating. At worst we become resigned and simply put up with the status quo.

To determine whether we are responding or reacting we can ask, "For the sake of what are we responding?" If there is no intention or commitment behind our actions, then our actions are essentially automatic and thoughtless. If we are responsible for our circumstances and intentional in our responses, when we become dissatisfied, innovating comes naturally.

Leaders who are responsive rather than reactive are not blind to problems or to people's concerns, but are organizing their actions based on something else. They are not attempting to "fix" people or simply solve problems but keeping their eye on the intended outcomes or purposes for which they are working. For example, in the movie *Apollo 13*, there is a moment when a technical crisis threatens the lives of the astronauts. All technical options have been exhausted and there is no possibility they will survive. The "leader" in the film throws down a pile of all the "stuff" in the space capsule and makes an unreasonable demand for the engineers to "create" a solution where none exists. This response could not have happened if the leader had believed that the circumstances were fixed.

CHOOSING—ACCEPTING THE CIRCUMSTANCES

To choose is a step beyond owning and responding freely to circumstances. To choose implies a choice about the circumstances to which we are responding. The idea of choice is synonymous with the idea of acceptance where we acknowledge not only that things are the way they are, but that they should be the way they are...even when the circumstances are not what we would wish and may be assessed as very negative. This is a very different state of relating than either succumbing or rationalizing that e can't help the way things are. This state involves embracing the change and the circumstances.

This notion is very basic to many spiritual disciplines in both the East and the West; its premise is that we can experience enormous freedom when we acknowledge that "reality" is happening regardless of our point of view or understanding. In fact, we can even at some point notice that by the time our brains can "think" about what is happening in the moment, the moment is already past. Eckhart Tolle in his book *The Power of Now* shows that to choose is to learn to live in the present and to be present to whatever is happening. This experience is familiar to almost anyone who has participated in sports and been in "the zone," or to people in the performing arts who have transcended thinking about or controlling a performance and simply expressed themselves fully.

In this state of choosing or "being present" we becomes different observers. We can observe all sorts of possibilities and choices that otherwise would remain buried in the circumstances. This is a state in which innovation is natural and effortless, even obvious. It is important to note, however, that this is also a state in which the circumstances are still "out there" and the observer is still relating to the world as something separate and distinct from the observer.

This is the state where leadership begins to become an increasingly creative process. This is also where we can observe a paradox between fully accepting the way things are without any resistance whatsoever and simultaneously creating a commitment to a larger possibility. In this context it is obvious that possibilities are by definition created, and leadership is about creating vision and possibility in relationship with other human beings.

BRINGING FORTH—CREATING THE CIRCUMSTANCES

This way of relating to the world and to circumstances is the state that we normally associate with truly "creative" people. What I wish to distinguish here is that the ability to create something is not a "gift" that a few especially endowed people have inherited. While it is true that some people come by this capacity "naturally," it is a learnable way of relating to the world, and the creative expressions it makes available begin to approach what we earlier distinguished as breakthroughs. To "bring forth" means not only to choose a circumstance that is already occurring, but to begin to relate to the world "as if" we are creating the circumstances themselves.

This is not necessarily a strange or metaphysical notion. We have known in the field of quantum mechanics for some time that everything we perceive is constantly being changed in the process of being perceived. The noted physicist John Wheeler, in an interview with *Discover* magazine (June 2002), has suggested that even the fact of the existence of an objective universe itself might be viewed as a product of our capacity to consciously observe and distinguish a world that only appears separate from us.

In an organizational context, for example, most of us have experienced or witnessed moments of sudden and often profound insight into the nature of a situation or circumstance and have formulated what seem to be (and often are) genuinely original ideas or solutions. In retrospect these innovations or inventions can be seen as: a) unpredictable, b) requiring challenge or change to some underlying belief or assumption about what is and is not possible, and c) generally obvious after the fact. A classic example is the story from the 3M Corporation about the invention of the Post-It that was created when a project looking for stronger glue failed. The inventor "brought forth" a new interpretation of what was wanted and needed (removable notes) and which bad glue could provide.

The point is that this insight required a different order of creative thinking outside conventional and reasonable frames of reference…what is usually meant by "outside the box" thinking. The question here is whether anyone can learn to be creative simply by beginning to change how he or she relates to the circumstances. I believe that this is possible and in fact is how most people develop what might be described as creative talent. To do so, however, requires that we let go of our notion that we are objects in an objective world and adopt a worldview in which we are individually and collectively creating the circumstances that we are observing.

Leaders who "bring forth" are those we normally consider to be "visionary" and charismatic and who are often seen as gifted in their capacity to keep moving forward and creating openings for action regardless of the circumstances. In Shakespeare's *Henry V,* the king gives an impassioned speech to his soldiers in the face of insurmountable odds. In doing so, he not only creates a possibility where none exists, but inspires his army to victory. For the leader who relates to the world in this way, a vision is not a big goal or picture of the future, but a powerful ground of being from which to create reality.

MASTERY—CREATING THE CONTEXT FOR CHANGE

"To create" here means to distinguish the rare ability that a few people have demonstrated to invent entirely new fields of inquiry.

These people are creating new domains, new openings, and new possibilities for others to explore and innovate. This is working at a different level and is a very distinct way of relating to circumstances in which the "creator" is the author of the context in which the creator is relating. To create a context means to be responsible not only for what is being perceived, not only for one's responses, not only for a generative relationship to the circumstances, but to be responsible for creating the background or space within which the circumstances appear.

"Mastery" of anything from art to penmanship is ultimately mastery of oneself and "who one is being" in a situation and in relationship to the world. Hence, to become a master of innovation, we must own both what is happening as well as what isn't happening...to be present to both "what is" as well as to the cognitive and transparent boundaries that define our perceivable reality.

In 1980 a man named Fernando Flores wrote a PhD thesis titled "Management and Communication in the Office of the Future" (UC Berkley, 1980). In his thesis he asked this simple question: "What is action for a manager?" His thesis opened an entirely new view of management as a phenomenon that happens in conversations, and that action occurs as "speaking and listening." His work has transformed much contemporary thinking about how coordination occurs in organizations and has impacted thinking and practices in the fields of information technology, artificial intelligence, health care, international relations, and development of leaders, among others. Where this will go remains to be seen, but his work illustrates creating a new meta-paradigm for observing, not simply making different observations in the same paradigm. When we are the creators of the paradigm or context, then we can begin to consider that we are in fact creating and mastering our circumstances.

Finally, leadership in a context of mastery is often very modest and may seem effortless or so natural as to appear inconsequential at the time. Mahatma Gandhi, for example, was a gentle man who used no force, and yet showed us how not resisting can be a powerful force for change. His mastery did not even seem to be leadership for most of his career, and yet from the beginning he was pursing the creation of a new reality. In addition, leaders who live and work in this context are constantly inventing or creating their experience. In this sense they are always beginners, learning and creating in each moment.

SUMMARY

Innovation happens at different levels from modest improvements on an existing product or process to dramatic and even historically significant breakthroughs in how we relate to the world. In all cases, the capacity to innovate will be a function of our commitments and concerns—what we want to accomplish and our relationship with the circumstances we perceive we are in. If we are resisting or coping, we see no innovation and whatever change we generate will be as a reaction to the

circumstances and part of the process by which those circumstances persist. When we are responding or choosing, we are
in a position to innovate and will do so naturally and consistently as a function of what we observe to be possible or what
we observe is missing in our perspective of the world. Change
based on this view is likely to be an improvement on what
already exists. When we are bringing forth or creating we are
not only in a position to innovate but are predisposed to do so.
Further, in these ways of relating to circumstances, we have few
if any limitations on what we can imagine and generate; we are
likely to be generating breakthroughs or even creating entirely
new spheres of possibility.

I consider leaders and innovators as those who are concerned with and competent at bringing "new realities" into
existence. I consider innovating to be a primary element in the
process of leading, and I see innovations as examples of leadership results or outcomes.

The following is a table that summarizes the six ways of
relating to change associated with different leadership models,
intentions and views of circumstances.

	Resisting	Coping	Responding	Choosing	Bringing Forth	Mastery
Leadership Model	Soldier	Facilitator	Father/ Teacher/ Mentor	Coach	Charismatic	Gifted Genius
Intention	Survive	Thrive	Be Responsible	Be Serene	Create Circumstances	Create Possibility
View of Circumstance	Fixed/ Deterministic	Fixed/ Not Deterministic	Fixed/ Choice of how we relate	Not Fixed/ Commitment to accept	Not Fixed/ Commitment to create circumstance	Not Fixed/ Commitment to create context
Example of Innovation	None	Technology for avoiding unwanted communication (e.g. spam)	Non Violent Advocacy	Alcoholics Anonymous	U.S. Constitution	Quantum Mechanics

FIGURE A

CHAPTER 4

MANAGERS ANONYMOUS

with Roger Evered

We are in increasing danger of acting as if we knew what we were doing, when we don't; and then not being able to bear the consequences of having erred.

—Robert Biller, 1969

American managers in the late 1980s had a certain way of interpreting the job of managing, a way so ingrained and habitual that on the whole we don't realize it's an interpretation—not until we look at the practice of American managers in, say, the 1930s, or at the turn of the century. A comparison with Japanese, Mexican, or Swedish managers exposes even more telling differences. In fact, it's only by noticing how "unusual" their practices are that we can define our own. Like fish, we have difficulty seeing that we are "swimming" in a management pond made up of unexamined assumptions and beliefs. We believe that as managers we can be far more effective than we are at present. But to do that, we have to change the way we think about management. And to change, we first have to be aware of our current habits, of the culture-bound and largely unconscious assumptions that determine the way we see the world. The consequences of acting from habit rather than conscious thought are that we are not really responsible either for our actions or for the results those actions produce. In effect, we are addicted to our own view of the world, and to the patterns of thought and action permitted by that view.

We do not use the word *addicted* for effect or as a metaphor. We actually mean addicted.

The problems managers work on are a function of interpretation, and managers are addicted to their interpretations. If we can break our addiction, we can break the condition that underlies and perpetuates our corporate problems.

When we think of addiction, we normally think of addiction to substances, although sometimes we think of addiction to some particular behavior. Only rarely do we notice that people can be powerfully addicted to an idea, or a belief, or a worldview constituted primarily of a set of beliefs and assumptions. For example, the problems of America's declining productivity and competitiveness could be the product of a national addiction to a particular way of viewing the world.

In effect, we are addicted to our own view of the world, and to the patterns of thought and action permitted by that view.

A PARADOX

Most of us have known people we would describe as unmistakably addicted—to alcohol, work, sex, gambling, or something else. Addicted people appear irresponsible. They have been unable to stop doing whatever it is they are addicted to, even when it obviously harms them and those around them. They function with considerable difficulty and behave weirdly on occasion. They are often defensive and unable to listen, have memory lapses, rationalize their behavior, blame others, and are likely to become belligerent when confronted by the seemingly obvious.

Above all, they deny the problem and seem completely unaware of their role in generating the problem. They just do not see themselves as causing the difficulties they must cope with. They refuse—or abuse—help you offer, and at some point become untrustworthy. You might say they are their own worst enemies.

THE PRINCIPLES OF ADDICTION

The first principle of any addiction is that "it" has power over the person's behavior. That's what distinguishes a habit from an addiction. Addicts think they can choose to stop, but actually "it" plays the tune to which they dance. The ability to choose is only recovered when the addiction is acknowledged and dealt with as such.

But addicts must maintain a facade of control. They must protect themselves from knowing that their addiction is out of control, that their behavior is generating destructive consequences, and that their addiction is the source of the difficulties in their lives. They must keep their relationship to "the problem" totally outside their awareness.

To do this, they must rely on four defensive mechanisms:

- Denial: what problem?
- Rationalization: reasons, explanations, and justifications for what happened
- Projection: others are unreliable, unfair, troublemaking
- Memory Distortions: euphoric recall and selective forgetting

As long as these mechanisms are operating, it is nearly impossible for addicts to recognize their disease and the need for recovery. Does this description fit anyone you have encountered in organizational settings? That is, does the description of an addict fit the managerial behavior of any managers you have known at work?

IS THIS YOUR ORGANIZATION?

Let's illustrate the point. We know a large, well-known, traditional organization that's a gold mine of managerial and organizational problems. The organization is compliance driven and places a high value on authority as the key to its effectiveness. Most people in the organization know that the organization could be much more productive and effective, as well as a more satisfying place to work. Almost everyone has an explanation of what's wrong with the place and who ought to do what to put it right. Gossip abounds in the hallways, cafeterias, and carpools. Denial is rampant. Some things that need to be said are never said, and some crucial questions are never asked, such as why certain meaningless activities are perpetuated.

The organization promotes the facade that it's well run, but everyone knows it's a joke. Nobody is really responsible.

In the contemporary culture of management, managers are addicted to a set of assumptions about people and how to manage them.

Managers can't stop the unproductive behavior because—given the underlying assumptions—it appears that they're doing the right thing.

Problems in this organization usually surface as crises, and upper management's response is something like "Find the cause of the problem and fix it!" Task forces are frequently assembled, although their recommendations are rarely implemented. More often, someone is appointed to carry out yet another study of the people at the lower levels, since the theory is that the lower levels are what the upper levels are supposed to manage. Conversely, those at the lower levels are certain that upper management is the source of the productivity problems and organizational difficulties. Nobody takes responsibility for the state of affairs. It is not apparent to anyone that the entire scenario is perpetuated by a set of assumptions about people, organizations, work, and management.

ADDICTION TO ASSUMPTIONS

These assumptions, most of them long forgotten, comprise everyday truths and conventional wisdom. For example, when an employee's job performance doesn't meet the boss's expectations, the boss has an immediate interpretation of the employee's performance, frequently formed without consulting the employee or anyone else. Only rarely will he or she consider an alternative interpretation of the event.

Or consider the common practice of keeping certain information, such as salary increases, secret. Even when these everyday managerial "truths" and conventional organizational "wisdom" don't produce the desired outcomes (better employee job performance, for example), managers continue to operate within them.

HITTING BOTTOM

One of the distinguishing characteristics of addicts is that denial of the addiction often continues until they hit bottom. It is nearly impossible for addicts to recognize their disease—and the need for treatment—until they hit bottom. When the alcoholic hits bottom, he or she may lose spouse, job, house, friends. When a manager hits bottom, he or she may lose staff, reputation, customers, profits, organization, career, self-esteem, and ethical integrity.

Many American managers seem well on their way to hitting bottom. Some are fortunate enough to have already hit bottom (as any recovered addict knows, hitting bottom is often the gateway to recovery).

MANAGERISM AND ITS SYMPTOMS

The name we've given to this particular addiction is "managerism." Managerism has many faces: low productivity and poor profitability, excessive rules and regulations, confusion and crises, job stress and workaholism, gossip and gamesmanship, dishonesty and disinformation, absenteeism and turnover, alienation and apathy.

Managerism is an addictive disease in which managers believes themselves to be in charge of their actions, while in fact their actions derive from the background of unnoticed assumptions. What probably best characterizes American managerism is the unspoken belief that everything in the organization can and should be controlled.

What are the other unspoken principles that American managers live by? As far as we know, no systematic work has attempted to identify them, but we can make a pretty good guess based upon our experience with American managers and our reading of the business press. The list below offers some examples of the unspoken rules,

or background principles, of American managerism. They should be sufficiently recognizable as "pollutants" of the managerial pond in which we are swimming.

There seems to be a growing recognition of the unacceptability of these symptoms, which, as we have argued, derive from managerism—an addiction truly detrimental to the health of organizations and the economy. The bottom line is that managers and organizations increasingly dedicate themselves to maintaining their current operations, to surviving the immediate crises, to perpetuating themselves, to justifying their existence. They lose the capacity to see possibilities that might generate a different future from the one that would automatically occur from the drift of events.

UNSPOKEN RULES UNDERLYING THE DISEASE OF AMERICAN MANAGERISM

- Take care of #1.
- Get turf, mark it, and build strong alliances to keep it.
- Keep winning in the short run.
- Every problem has a cause: find it and fix it.
- Justify everything.
- Be careful, minimize risk, hedge your bets, don't rock the boat.
- People are only useful if they do what you want them to do.
- Cover your ass, take credit, avoid blame (and always know who to blame).
- Cheap, quick fixes are better than costly solutions.

- People have got to be motivated, whether by a carrot or stick.
- Rank has its privileges.
- Don't lose control. Act as if you know what you're doing, especially if you suspect you don't.
- People are cost factors. Everyone is expendable except me—and maybe you.
- Develop allies in powerful places, stay ahead of your peers at all costs, and don't get too close to the people you work with.
- Never admit you screwed up. Punish errors in others.
- Don't trust. Keep the important stuff secret.
- Always look good.

MANANON

How can we prevent managers/addicts from further damaging themselves, their friends, their organizations, and the economy? What can be done to minimize the suffering and ineffectiveness of people at work?

Consider, if you will, a nationwide network of recovery treatment centers to deal with the disease of managerism. Now that more and more managers are hitting bottom, there's a need for readily accessible recovery centers, located in or near the major corporate zones, which can provide self-help treatment for this addiction. We propose to call the organization Managers Anonymous, or ManAnon.

The only requirement for membership is an acknowledgement of one's addiction to managerism and a clear intention to recover from it. ManAnon would operate with the well-known Twelve Step Program that has been so successful in treating a variety of other addictions, beginning with alcoholism. Our version of AA's first three steps for managerism is:

1. We admitted we were powerless over our assumptions about organization, management, and work, and that our organizations had become unworkable.
2. We came to see that a managerial context larger than ourselves could restore us to sanity.
3. We made a decision to commit our will and our work lives to a worthy organizational vision.

American managers aren't going to shake their bad habits until they quit denying that they're addicted to the old management.

CHAPTER 5

EFFECTIVE RELATIONSHIPS: RETHINKING THE FUNDAMENTALS

It is axiomatic that nothing that has been made, or may be made, is possible outside a context of effective and true human relationships. In any organization committed to total quality, relationships are necessary to get the work done. In fact, the ability to establish and maintain functional relationships that generate effective networks among people is one of the key capabilities expected from the personnel of an organization and the cultural transformations it is committed to achieve.

In the field of management change, there are methodologies and patterns that have assumed for a long time that human dimensions in the organization are fundamental, although they have been getting little or no attention at all. Many processes focused on people's "sensitivity" were attempted, and some produced good results in relation to the setting up of working teams. *All of them proved to be very useful in the short-term and lacked exhaustive theoretical or intellectual research to be sustainable over time or applicable to a large number of people over long periods of time.*

The need to have a discipline to distinguish between generative and explanatory principles—if the objective was to achieve the organizational transformation—has been acknowledged. It is understood that "trust" is a critical issue. A discipline is needed to *instill* confidence, not only a better understanding of the lack of confidence or the reasons for not trusting others.

In no way does this understanding bring about a utopian state of relationship. It is necessary to work daily on relationships within the organization. In fact, in the same way that views and commitments grow, breakdowns may grow, too. This is inevitable and healthy at the same time: it indicates that the really deep patterns and negative behavior mechanisms are reaching the surface, are becoming evident. These mechanisms are typically hidden, buried in bureaucratic resignation; they frequently hold back the best intentions for change. Anyway, what is significant is that *breakdowns* in relationships are no longer considered as if relationships were unchangeable, nor are they papered over with excuses.

On the contrary, practices are developed related to the posing of key questions on what constitutes a "good relation"; i.e., which are the individual commitments and how we must continue developing abilities to constantly improve effective relationships.

Receiving ever greater recognition is the fact that issues related to communication within a company cannot be separated from general communication issues, which are the same thing...like the two sides of the same coin. Every issue is related to conventional wisdom, the clichés and the folklore of the organization. The practices to develop relationships and a committed communication are equivalent to the organization's view of the future that is still not evident. Until the total quality issue was developed in the world, people did not confront the deep and philosophical personal questions that have historically limited their capacity to think creatively and to *design* relationships.

WHAT IS AN ORGANIZATION?

In the context of this discussion the first question should be "what is an organization?" When posing this question, the perfect definition or the correct answer has not yet been given. Actually, what is required is an answer providing a way of observing the organization so as to allow the creation of new possibilities of invention and design. For example, any company may be considered as a group of human beings related to one another and coordinating actions to produce a common future.

The patterns, structures, and practices of company management come from the past and may not have changed since the past century. Management philosophy as we know it, and its related practices, has its origin in military practice, where a command and its control systems make sense. Before the midpoint in the nineteen hundreds, as the change very slowly was taking place, people had few options; an orientation based on control and proceedings worked reasonably well.

In the environment, where organizations currently exist, change is not constant and is accelerating in virtually all fields.

The complexity of organizations and systems is observed as a primary source of anxiety and stress among the people responsible for their operation. In spite of all the studies carried out during these years, and after twenty years of sophisticated information technology, our basic context within management continues to be the intention to control human behavior in order to optimize working results and procedures through the exercise of authority. The traditional ways of observing work in general as well as teamwork in particular must be analyzed in the light of improvements carried out in the fields of human communication and management.

RELATIONSHIPS AND COMMUNICATION

Organizational design has traditionally stressed building facilities, the organizational structure in which roles and authority are outlined and finally, the information processes and materials defining the tasks and procedures to be carried out. Although all of these aspects are important, none of them is focused on how people will communicate and relate, nor do they provide the bases for integrating the organizational design with the vision, the commitment, and the statement of customer satisfaction, according to the mutual satisfaction conditions agreed upon.

To better approach this issue, we must examine the basic interpretation of "who we are" as individuals and as part of the community. Furthermore, we must ask ourselves within our being and the culturally imposed limits regarding the personal action of the individual and his or her responsibility which determines the frontiers of *what is* possible and *what is not* possible in the future. Success in reaching the goals set is achieved through relationships with others. The future is constantly created through conversations with others—asking and creating commitments, making requests and promises through actions. From this perspective, commitments are actions. The successful coordination of relationships is the coordination of commitments expressed in the acts of language.[1]

If we notice how people reach agreements on what is important, what makes sense, and what works or does not work, it is evident that they do so on the basis of assertions and assessments. Considering our common sense, most people believe that their assessments are perfect descriptions of reality. Explanations and points of view focused on right and wrong are anchored in this point of view. Although it is more difficult, it is more useful and powerful to consider assessments and assertions as acts of language, and as commitments with an interpretation of "how things are," and not as a fact, in the case of assertions.

All conversations take place against a background of commitments focused on the past, the present, or the future. This point of view offers a new interpretation of the interactions that take place within an organization, that provide possibilities not seen until that time, and that coordinate human actions in the organization.

The first challenge is to develop the basic abilities to observe, communicate, and relate to others within a context of commitment. The next challenge is to redesign the organization and the working processes to allow people to effectively navigate within their network of relationships in the organization.

A NEW DISCIPLINE FOR MANAGEMENT AND DESIGN

Human beings coordinate actions in the context of their relationships and through described conversation processes, such as committed speaking and listening.

---

1.   Dr. F. Flores, 1982.

When doctors prescribe an analysis, they are not only sending information to another department but are also making a request for someone to comply with certain *conditions* of *satisfaction* within a *given time frame*. The doctor is satisfied if the correct result is complied with in the specified period of time.

Technology and the technicians' abilities are strict means to achieve that purpose. The doctor is a client asking for a service, and the technician makes the promise to satisfy the conditions of satisfaction of that order.

Successful coordination requires that both parties understand and agree on this basic relation. The work will not be complete until the doctor/customer is satisfied. The failure in the production of satisfactory results originates resentment, resignation, and loss of confidence; it may eventually reinforce a mechanistic organizational culture, based on procedures and control oriented. Human beings cease to be possibilities for others, and even worse, they become "the problem."

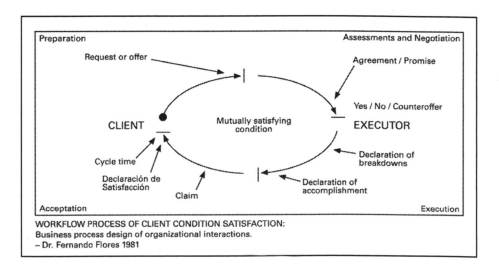

WORKFLOW PROCESS OF CLIENT CONDITION SATISFACTION:
Business process design of organizational interactions.
– Dr. Fernando Flores 1981

Figure B

The figure B shows the basic structure that explains every situation or process among two or more human beings. This is called *basic action process of workflow* or *process design of the organizational interaction business*. These processes and concepts constitute the minimum and necessary distinctions to design any process or the development of management practices for effective action coordinated within the company.

BASIC ACTION PROCESS OF WORKFLOW

The diagram of the basic action of the workflow process may be considered as a basic structure map to observe the coordination of actions among persons. This representation, universally observable, is an constitutive aspect of the human enterprise. It suggests there is no intentional occurrence until someone makes a request or an offer so that certain condition of satisfaction may be met.

A condition of satisfaction is the *criterion* to satisfy a commitment by the person making a request or an offer. It should be noticed that that condition of satisfaction is always implied in any request or offer and is usually construed in a context of shared traditions and practices. For example, if someone orders a cup of coffee in the United States, there is no need to say that it should be hot and with no milk, unless you specifically order it with milk and cold. In another culture, such as France, the implicit satisfaction condition of that same request includes milk or cream.

In every workflow two roles are always included. One is the client, whose conditions of satisfaction must be fulfilled, and the other is the work force, whose commitment is the client's satisfaction. After a client makes an order or an offer (which is an observable act of language), the client and the supplier (the doer) negotiate until the supplier commits itself to meet the conditions of satisfaction or agrees upon the offer. Using this structure of interpretation it is evident, for example, how often the executives within an organization make requests or offers assuming their acceptance when that agreement hasn't actually been reached. Focusing on the specific acts of language or on the commitments in each phase of the basic action process of workflow, ambiguity, mistaken comprehension, and subsequent breakdowns are significantly reduced or avoided. Furthermore, when bad coordination occurs, we need only to analyze the cause, correct it, and carry on.

Upon reaching an agreement, the conditions of satisfaction are "mutual" and produced by the supplier. This stage is completed by a statement—another act of language—that states that "the work is done." The coordination is not complete until the client declares, "Yes, you satisfied my conditions of satisfaction. Thank you." Unless these basic acts are fulfilled, there is always uncertainty, a potential dissatisfaction and expense, together with the personal tension, bad mood, and disagreement that are common in organizational relationships.

The basic action process of workflow represents a simple act of coordination. Actually, each institutional process is a workflow that has many clients and many suppliers.

What has been proven to be of great value is to have a common language and the same coordination structure on many levels, from the relationships of the company with its clients and intermediate processes with which a client feels satisfied, up to individual coordination within a unit or a department.

The observation of a series of procedures or control activities of the material movement or data is made easy by observing the work from this perspective. This structure not only enables its members to understand the concept of human coordination but also to observe expenditure from a new perspective.

Expenditure occurs for a number of reasons and takes different forms. In contemporary society, expense or loss is generally seen in material or physical terms. Organizations generally tend to reduce expenditure with technology, increasing the levels of organizational complexity. This usually leads to useless efforts and creates a "downward spiral" where any intended improvement is impossible to carry out. Even more important, in companies where most of the work is service oriented, this form of eliminating or reducing expenses or loss implies more red tape and self-justification.

For example, it is frequently heard that doctors increase the costs of medicine by requiring many analyses and procedures that are clinically unnecessary. The attempts to find a solution have included new polices, control systems, committee review procedures, training, and others. Nevertheless, most professionals agree that this continues to be a significant source of loss and expense in many institutions.

Why do attempts to change this fail, when the general agreement is that the change is necessary and beneficial? An answer might be that people have misunderstood the problem and therefore are looking for a solution that not only makes no difference but creates more problems and a negative mood.

Instead of looking at the problem as "unnecessary procedures," we may consider the possibility that the problem is lack of coordination and trust among the various participants in the institution, combined with an insufficient commitment to clarify and satisfy the conditions of a particular request. From this perspective, the loss or expense is considered an opportunity to build relationships and create innovation, a commitment, and clear communication.

Loss and expense occur when within the relation people don't clearly see the conditions of satisfaction or commitments, when a basic action process of workflow is incomplete, or when the roles are confused. This loss takes the shape of delays, confusion, dissatisfaction, relation breakdowns, and unnecessary or redundant actions.

COMMITTED COMMUNICATION

Every communication involves speech, either oral or written, or through some other electronic means. Communication is not only the transfer of information or data; it also involves listening. Listening isn't "hearing" the information passively; it is an active and interpretative action, based on the observer's competences, his or her history, culture, and commitments in relation to the people involved in the conversation.

In human networks that encompass an organization, its executives must speak and understand the same language. In the same way that they need to share linguistic distinctions related to their work, it is also important that they share basic distinctions for the effective coordination of everyday conversations. There are five linguistic distinctions through which human coordination takes form, and they are outlined in the work carried out by Fernando Flores (1982): declarations, requests/offers, promises, judgments, and assertions.

DECLARATIONS

Declarations are acts of speech that generate a different reality in the world. They are made by those who have the authority to speak in the name of a community of people. Declarations are commitments that turn out to be possibilities and/or facts at the time of speaking (e.g., "I declare you husband and wife"). They can be made by a less-formal person, such as Gandhi declaring India independent from England, or, for example, an executive declaring that his or her team will be the best in the corporation. Statements generate new realities, and the actions of the person making the declaration are consistent with what has been said or the new reality that has been declared.

REQUESTS/OFFERS

Request and offers are commitments that require that an action be carried out within a certain period of time; they are related to a certain condition of satisfaction. They create the *future*. A request is not a wish; it requires an answer that can be an acceptance (a promise), a rejection, or a counteroffer (e.g., "I ask you to do this work, in less time with the same resources, starting next week").

PROMISES

Promises are commitments to carry out an action that has been requested, in the future. They require fulfilling or performing mutual conditions of satisfaction. An unrequested promise is an offer that will be conditioned to being accepted by somebody else. Promises can be revoked. In that case the person must be responsible for the consequences of this action and its effects on the relation with the others, or must, in certain cases, pay a compensation, (e.g., "I promise that I will make a change by next Saturday and that I'll let you know when it's done").

JUDGMENTS

Judgments are declarations. They are statements made by someone as an interpretation of a fact for the later coordination

77

of an action or to open new possibilities. When made with responsibility, judgments are always specific within a certain sphere, relative with regard to a standard, and may or may not be validated by assertions or facts. Judgments are neither true nor false and always live in the person making them; they may share consensus with another person, but are never true or false. The speaker's commitment is to support the judgment if required (e.g., "We can improve the quality of our services").

ASSERTIONS

Assertions are defined as statements made by the speaker that are a fact and may be verified by another observer or by witnesses. The speaker's commitment is to provide evidence if required. A statement may be true or false, but it can always be verified through an independent observation, if challenged (e.g., "We are $x under the budget"). The speaker's commitment is to provide evidence.

CONCLUSION

With these basic distinctions of the acts of speech, people learn to listen generously to the opportunities to coordinate in a more effective manner and are also capable of observing instances in which there is a breakdown in coordination. Moreover, new questions such as "what are we having this conversation for" are starting to take the place of other, old, common answers, such as having to justify oneself or defend a point of view. To speak and listen in a committed way isn't a panacea, or the best conceivable thing. But they are the basis for bringing to the surface and solving breakdowns fast, building relationships and trust, and observing how human beings coordinate commitments. This interpretation does not replace the need for effective management of materials and information systems but vastly simplifies its design and implementation.

CHAPTER 6

PROSPER WITH VISION

I started my career as a consultant working with governmental organizations in 1969, when computers filled large basements and were a great promise for those of us who were interested in efficiency and effectiveness. During the following ten years, I devoted myself exclusively to projects in the public sector and worked on a wide range of programs that dealt with health care and social services, the legislative and environmental areas, public works, and security, with economic development and the executive branch in the US government. I met and got to know many professionals of local, state, and federal public services in the US and Canada.

We were young, committed, and enthusiastic, and I enjoyed a good salary. I believed that true change was possible and that we could make the difference in the quality of life of our communities and for people in general. In the mid seventies, some of us who took management and corporate issues seriously became disappointed. I started to ask myself if the reorganizations, studies, new systems, training programs, and more idealistic policies made any difference.

For all our "understanding," clever models, and organizational efforts, it seemed that individuals (government employees and institutions) were very similar to what they had been before. They wanted to improve their situation, but they had a deep sense of frustration—struggling to make big changes, but more or less resigned. We began to believe that it was not possible to go against the cultural "realities" of bureaucratic organizations to implement fundamental changes.

I realized that this condition was not limited to the public sector—that it had invaded large companies everywhere. My clients and I were on board the same ship; we either resigned ourselves to believe that it was not possible to make a real difference in large bureaucracies or fell into cynicism and despair. The only option left was to undertake a certain type of research we hadn't considered, to discover or create another possibility that wasn't obvious; to start seriously questioning our most basic assumptions and inquire into what was missing or what needed to be invented in order to achieve a qualitative change in organizational culture.

We needed to learn if corporate transformation was possible and if so, how to make it a reality.

To make this story short, this inquiry had me, and others, beginning to question ourselves and try a variety of nonconventional approaches to large-scale corporate change, beginning from distinguishing the "culture" of the company and "searching for excellence" by the end of the seventies, to various strategies for enhancing "performance" such as "self-managing" teams, "appreciative inquiry," and "total quality" in the eighties and subsequent years. More recently we've undertaken substantial investments in "reengineering" business processes, creating "paradigm shifts" and designing "learning organizations."

What do you think when you listen to these terms? I believe that many people hear these terms as management fads, good advice, tips and techniques, tricks for consultants to get rich, new words for common sense, or, even worse, as another opportunity to have your hopes dashed—followed by more disappointment and resignation. This is not to say these approaches don't yield benefits; they often do. But the benefits are often short-term, and they all seem to fall short of delivering a qualitative shift, a transformation of the organizational culture. They generally fail to consistently deliver breakthroughs in people's ability to perform and their experience of what is possible.

Beyond all these words we can see at least two things in common. First: all of them start with the point of view that "business as usual" is not acceptable and that significant investments are required to change the way we work *and* the prevailing "mindset" if we are to prosper in an increasingly uncertain future. Second: the starting point for virtually every strategy for large-scale organizational change is some *vision* of a desired future that we want.

I believe that most everyone has done personal and direct work and has life experience in the context of a vision, at some time in your life. I believe that it was a time when you were inspired, energized, confident, creative, enthusiastic, maybe courageous and deeply involved with your colleagues. Do you remember having such experiences in your career—a golden moment, a great project, a period in which you were inspired by the possibility of achieving a breakthrough?

This is the "way of being" that I want you to use as a point of reference. It is a way of being in which we experience

83

flourishing in the context of a vision. Let me ask you another question: have you experienced a corporate exercise of developing a vision, but after all the discussions and exchange of words the vision was buried in a drawer together with other planning exercises and nice words? It becomes something that we all agree should happen, but it lacks the power to sustainably move us to change our lives or the reality of our organization.

Since many of us have had such experiences, I would ask you to think about yourself as a human being and how we think about and experience vision. My objective is not to give you the answer or the "how." I prefer to share some of the results and conclusions of our research to make you think and to stimulate you, and maybe to open new possibilities for you and your organization. I consider as a given that without a bold vision and extraordinary action, the future of your company will be an extension of the past and "business as usual." To begin, I want to look at vision from three perspectives:

- What is a vision, and why, when we think we have developed one, do we often fail to take the action needed to make it reality?
- What distinctions and ideas have we found to be useful when moving to bring a vision into reality—how is this reality supported and what we can observe about how human beings create their future through communication?
- Do we have a common vision, and if not, some thoughts about our common future?

WHAT IS A VISION?

I believe that part of the difficulty we experience when producing a powerful vision is that we do not make a distinction between understanding the vision as a "big goal or objective" and seeing it as the "future as possibility." This confusion

84

results in a either relating to the vision as "out there"—as a future state—or seeing it more powerfully as a ground of being—a place to come from, not a destination. A vision, when it has the power of vision, becomes our raison d'être today. A vision lives as a deep and profound personal commitment to a possible future. The key is in understanding that possibilities do not exist in reality; they are by definition not real, but occur as a context for our relationship to the future in the present.

For example, most of us could easily agree with a vision for our department or organization, such as "being a world class leader in providing services to the public…blah blah blah." Who would be against this? However, as an objective for future design, it assumes that this is not the way it is today. The current context for action is that we are not there, and many will understand this kind of language to be idealistic—few will bet their pension on it happening. The vision, while desirable, is too general, not seen a real possibility; and more importantly, our actions will always be consistent with who we are now and not who we can be. So for a vision to have power, we must be committed that the vision is already "the way it is" as a possibility for it to impact action in the present.

The second point I want to share here is that the vision does not exist as a "thing." It is a human phenomenon that exists only in daily conversations with other people. We can write it down, but the written or spoken content is not the same as when the vision lives as a commitment, a declaration. A vision is not a concept or a model for the future, just as an architect's scheme is not the same as the structure that the architect's "sees" emerging from the work of the contractor. We have all grown up and been educated in a worldview in which we tend to objectify everything. A vision is not an object and it is not a

human beings with common interests. Haven't you realized that when children play they say something like:

"What do we have to do?"
"I don't know…let's play we are people from space!"
"OK, and let's pretend we are traveling to planet Boris."
"That's great, I think Boris people think with their feet"
"OK, then we have to move our heels to talk to them"
"Come on, let's do it!"

I think it is clear that children are not limited by "reality" when they create games. They may be informed by reality, but reality never limits them. To create a vision, a dialogue should also include the idea of "come on!" and "let's…" In fact, that is not a bad way of thinking about vision: a game we have created to play together. A successful conversation to create a vision starts with something someone imagines possible, and then others start to talk and listen collectively about what may be seen or imagined from that point of view. I am not merely talking about a brainstorming session or exercise but rather to actively create the possibility of the vision itself in the dialogue.

At a certain time, people discover that creating a vision is not about troubleshooting and turning life and work to normal. On the contrary, its value lies in developing a context through which uncertainty may be managed and new paths may be walked. A vision does not predict nor prescribe: it remains on the basis as a source of intention and direction; it does not guarantee a particular outcome. Let's consider Columbus's vision of arriving in the Far East by navigating to the West. His vision was enough to gain the trust of the monarchs, obtain substantial capital, keep men together when doubt arose, and finally discover a new world. But it never took him to the Far East.

Another aspect of creating a common and powerful vision is remembering that as in a marriage, the power and possibility of the vision arises from the commitment of people. It exists in the declarations of the people involved, and is inspiring for as long as the parties are creating the possibility, but can quickly becomes just a memory once the commitment changes. In other words, the vision must be continuously be regenerated if it is to exist as a source of inspiration and be sustainable over time. I like to think of a vision as being like a garden that becomes a living and growing possibility over time. Warren Bennis suggests that a leader must be a "gardener" for possibility and vision.

As vision emerges through creative dialogue for the future, it is important to remember that a vision does not change anything in the current reality. All of the same issues and problems persist, and most of our assessments about the status quo are unchanged. Vision transforms our *relationship* with reality; it gives us a new context from which to observe our situation and gives us a perspective from which we can make choices that we couldn't see before creating the vision. To keep a vision alive we must have competence and at least some distinctions about different areas of organizational life. Specifically we need to distinguish between what we are doing and our results and who we are or our ground of being. We should also distinguish that action is what determines the future—individual actions and collective actions. If we want a different future we must have a place to stand from which to take unprecedented actions. Finally we might distinguish that all of us do our work in one way or another through networks of people having conversations. From this perspective actions happen in conversations in the form of commitments expressed and fulfilled in the process of everyday coordination. We transform a vision into reality by coordinating actions and creating the future through committed communication.[2]

I will briefly explain what I mean by committed communication. As we have already said, a vision exists in the declarations of people. A declaration is a speech action in conversation. It is a commitment that something is possible before there is evidence that it exists. We all have the capacity and freedom to declare ourselves and in doing so declare a possible reality. Declarations produce an opening in a social context; some declarations may also require authority, such as when a referee in a game declares a penalty. Other declarations require only that human beings are authentic in their commitment, such as when one declares, "I love you" or "I am free." Whether the authority is guaranteed by the community or assumed by the individual, declarations only have the power to produce changes if those who make them are listened to as people with authority. If I ask, "Why did you get married?" the true answer is because the judge or the rabbi or the priest or another authority said so. If I ask, "Why did you follow that procedure?" the answer of the final analysis is because somebody said so. If I ask, "Why aren't you able to do something?" the final answer would be because you said so. A declaration is a kind of committed communication in which the context for the interpretation and the action is any context that you, me, or the community says.

Declarations do not produce action. They are only useful to define the purpose for the action. If we want something to happen, we do it through requests and promises. Most of us may consider that promises are commitments. If we observe,

---

2   Distinctions originally presented in PhD thesis "Management and Communication in the Office of the Future." Dr Fernando Flores. 1980.

we can see that a request is also a commitment—or at least it must be a commitment if we want our requests to be taken seriously—with which we are committed to obtain what has been requested. If you believe in this, ask your children to come back for dinner at six o'clock three nights in a row, and you be late. If you do not commit to accept and coordinate in a manner consistent with what you ask, people will stop taking your requests seriously.

Being a human being also means making assessments. People have opinions on everything and on everyone. The question is if you are committed to your assessment—not whether it is true or false, but whether you are committed to offering evidence for your reasoning so that others can have sufficient clarity with respect to what you are asking that they can choose to accept or decline the request or make a counter offer. "Our employees are not inspired because they don't understand our vision" is an assessment. It is an assessment of "reality" that cannot be proven in the sense of being observed or measured; and according to how it is interpreted by the listener, it may result in a resource commitment or simply be acknowledged as a point of view. In the context of committed communication, how we declare and how we listen to assessments will determine our possibilities and the openings we have for action.

Finally, we also can make assertions, a commitment that something may be observed by a third party as a fact. If I say that Ralph Klein is the premier of the Canadian Providence of Alberta, we can prove it as an assertion by looking at the election record. If I say he is a leader, that is an assessment. I can assert that the temperature is 25° C. I cannot assert that it is cold (or hot)—this would be an assessment.

This is a brief and inadequate orientation to an interpretation of business and management based on the emerging global vision that human beings are continuously creating new futures in conversations. As a consequence, the future does not need to be determined by the past. A vision of transforming the work in companies is possible when people are committed and create their vision with conviction.

But a vision and the commitment by themselves are only fantasy if they do not lead to action and new practices. Many new and effective practices already exist; they are generally on the margin: people who are trying nontraditional ways of working and relating. I encourage you to look for them and prove them for yourselves.

WHY IS THIS IMPORTANT?

Why are some of these notions are important? First of all, in today's world there are a few universal issues confronting us. Beyond the all publicized problems such as global warming, poverty, terrorism, and so forth, there is an underlying question of whether we have the capacity to resolve these and other issues. Is it possible to create a civilization that works for all of us? If not, we must resign ourselves that life and the state of affairs in the world are bigger than we are and do our best to survive in an increasingly complex and dangerous world. Without vision, without possibility, we are doomed to live in a "past-determined" reality and cope with circumstances as best we can. There are no problems or crises that cannot be resolved in a way that strengthens us and creates openings for even the most devastating circumstances to show us the way to greater and greater levels of accomplishment.

Second, as a practical matter our models for forecasting or predicting the future are breaking down. In most industries long-range planning is obsolete. At the rate knowledge is expanding, in some fields the latest book is obsolete before we read it. Even cherished notions such as "competition" or what a "job" is or even that there is a "right" recipe are being challenged as we experience the emergence of a new world that we understand or can comprehend. The overriding question facing most leaders today is "how do we navigate when we don't know where we are going?" The answer is that we have to navigate by our vision and allow what isn't working to give us the feedback we need to make course corrections. Any other strategy will inevitably force us into attempting to regain control and put us at grave risk of becoming obsolete ourselves as reality moves on. What got us to where we are is insufficient to help us prosper and thrive in the future.

Finally, it is our vision as a context that is always shaping our view of the future anyway. Moreover, our view of the future affects the choices we make and therefore our actions that in turn give us whatever the future will be. If we do not create a powerful vision for ourselves, our companies, and society, the default is that the past and what is predictable becomes our vision and will guarantee the persistence of business as usual.

CONCLUSION

In the final analysis, "vision" is only a word, and "prospering" is an assessment of our experience in work and life. To create a vision is the first step toward creating a new reality. Human beings create the future all the time through conversations. If we learn to listen and talk from our commitments and our vision, we will have the capacity of producing flexibility and satisfaction in spite of the circumstances—and perhaps one day a world that works for everyone.

CHAPTER 7

PASSING THE TORCH:
LEADERSHIP IN TRANSITION

These are unusual times for most organizations in the public sector. In the next several years, many senior personnel will be eligible to retire. Those who remain will take on new roles as part of normal executive rotations or may voluntarily leave the public service for other opportunities in the private or not-for-profit sectors. This situation is exceptional, not only because of the numbers and timeframes involved, but also because many others—not "just" senior people—are planning to retire or leave their jobs for other reasons. Voluntary turnover and downsizing in middle management matches the changes at higher levels, resulting in the possibility of people moving up two or three levels well in advance of where they would expect to under historical cycles for promotion. Last year Kevin Lynch said, "In this broader context, the demographics of the federal public service are ever more daunting. Fifteen years ago, federal employees in the 25-to-44-age cohort made up over 60% of the public service, with under 30% in the 45-to-64 cohort. Today, it is largely reversed with 50% of the public servants in the 45-to-64-age cohort, while just over 40% are in the 25-to-44-age cohort."[3]

THE CHALLENGE: PREPARING A GENERATION OF NEW LEADERS

As organizational leaders learned in both the public and private sectors during the massive downsizing of the eighties, large staff turnover can be extremely costly. After the fact, decision makers discovered they didn't really know what expertise and competencies were being lost, since much of it resided in people's "experience," not in their job descriptions, specialized knowledge, or process documentation.

In the September 2005 issue of *Canadian Government Executive*,[4] Brian Marson went so far as to suggest that the loss of experience and knowledge during this period can be likened to "organizational Alzheimer's." Aging in the public service is more prevalent in executive ranks: the average age of assistant deputy ministers is now fifty-three years, and the average age for all executives ranges from nearly fifty years (EX-1s) to fifty-two years (EX-3s). Twenty-six percent of executives today have at least thirty years of pensionable service, compared to

---

3   Remarks by the Clerk of the Privy Council, Canadian Council of Chief Executives (CCCE) National Policy Summit, *Public Policy and the Public Service Matter*, September 26, 2006.

4   http://www.networkedgovernment.ca/OrganizationalAlzheimersMarson

almost 10 percent of public servants overall.[5] Many government departments and agencies understand the strategic importance of addressing this unprecedented situation.

If this next generation of retirees takes responsibility for the future and the success of their successors and if the next generation of leaders accepts responsibility for getting what they need from today's leaders before they retire, then the stage will be set for achieving breakthroughs in the public service.

The real concern is that "we don't know what we don't know." The impacts of such rapid turnover are usually manifested in the form of unexpected (often unprecedented) problems and ethical issues resulting from blind spots and inexperience. In addition, organizations may need to hire back those who left at a premium, thereby incurring increased costs, or deal with reduced productivity and possibly deteriorating morale of a surviving workforce overwhelmed with work they are not equipped to handle.

How we prepare the next generation of leadership will set the stage for the next ten to fifteen years and will not only will impact employee engagement, productivity, and service levels, but also (for better or worse) the culture of the public service itself. If this next generation of retirees takes responsibility for the future and the success of their successors, and if the next generation of leaders accepts responsibility for getting what they need from today's leaders before they retire, then the stage will be set for achieving breakthroughs in the public service.

---

5   Remarks by the Clerk of the Privy Council, Canadian Council of Chief Executives (CCCE) National Policy Summit, *Public Policy and the Public Service Matter*, September 26, 2006.

TRADITIONAL APPROACHES

A variety of tools and approaches for accomplishing organizational transitions already exist—from training and development programs and succession planning to information-sharing, mentoring, and, occasionally, one-on-one coaching. Results vary considerably.

At best, these traditional efforts prepare new executives or managers with some background knowledge and help them begin the challenging process of establishing themselves in a new role. More often than not, learning the practical aspects of their new job starts from scratch when their predecessor exits. Competence and confidence levels may not reach those of their predecessor for some time (often a year or more), and lots of time is spent reinventing the wheel. Meanwhile, the accomplishment of the system as a whole remains more or less the same and may even diminish. In other cases, these approaches may develop technically competent managers capable of administering procedures and regulations. But having technical competence is not the same as being a leader capable of guiding the public service with the spirit, understanding, and sensibilities that come with experience and maturity.

Mentoring focuses on showing people the ropes, helping them see the potential in others, dealing with "the way it is," and sometimes going to bat for them or sponsoring them in some undertaking. Often, this been-there-done-that approach can be highly effective in preparing the next generation to deal with recurring or traditional tasks and issues. But it can be counterproductive in addressing unpredictable and often unprecedented challenges (unless the mentor is more of a coach engaged in co-creating responses in various situations).

Various schemes for transferring knowledge, whether through informal advisors, training programs, or online tools, can also be useful. However, mostly information-based tools and training are designed to teach procedures, processes, and policies. Some leadership training approaches effectively convey information relating to particular leadership models; however, none currently available focuses on those aspects of leadership having to do with developing the "qualitative" aspects of the individual. Moreover, even when the information that gets codified is excellent, it often doesn't get used or even heard in today's "information overload" world. For the kind of qualitative learning that is needed, the state-of-the-art remains the "apprenticeship model" combined with on-the-job experience. Unfortunately, most organizations lack the time and resources for this kind of natural and informal learning/ growth process to happen.

A BOLD DESIGN: ACCELERATED LEADERSHIP DEVELOPMENT

Accelerating the learning and maturity of the next generation of young leaders requires a different strategy, a more innovative and integrated approach than that currently offered by traditional training and mentoring models. This approach requires commitment from three parties within the organization:

1. *Top management must assume responsibility and be accountable for succession planning*—not consign it to the human resources function as an administrative concern. As one of their central concerns, the focus needs to be on the quality of the next generation's capacity for leadership in action and not be limited to evaluating resumes. (Imagine the level of conversations possible if executives and managers

received an "after retirement" bonus based upon the success of the next generation.)

We need to prepare the next generation of leaders to do more than just fill the shoes of those who will be retiring. What we need is for those who follow to stand on our shoulders and take the public service to an entirely new level of service and accomplishment.

2. ***Those retiring must be willing to consider that their legacy includes leaving the best of what they've learned***—especially the qualities and ways of being that have made the biggest difference. They must see themselves as responsible for the future and be willing to let go of their authority and any preconceived ideas of what things "should" look like. In many cases, the most important things we need to learn from our elders aren't even apparent to the elders—and they only become so when we open up to transfer the essence of who we are as leaders to our younger colleagues.

3. ***The next generation of leaders need to be willing to pull what they need from those who are retiring***—to mine the gold from them with all humility and engage in the process as leaders well in advance of actually being promoted to leadership roles. Instead of viewing themselves in terms of reinventing the wheel or filling someone's shoes, they must see their future role standing on the shoulders of their predecessors. A key difference between this approach and traditional models is that the younger generation must accept the necessity to be a leader first and then take the reins of authority as they mature. This is analogous to how young surgeons are trained: they are never told they are ready to cut into a human body. Instead, apprentice physicians declare they are ready by reaching for the blade. If older surgeons accept that apprentices are committed and prepared to be responsible for the outcomes of their actions, they

release the knife and the next level of learning and practice begins.

REAL-WORLD LEADERSHIP

In this new context, "passing the torch" focuses less on an individual's technical competencies and more on bringing about a fundamental shift in their "way of being." No formulas exist for what one needs to do or know to be a leader. Preparation and success depend upon relationship, commitment, and the opportunity to take on some challenge having real and tangible results that cannot be accomplished without demonstrating the intended leadership qualities.

Accelerating leadership development acknowledges that it is the generation of twenty-to-forty-year-olds that has the biggest stake in learning what they need to learn from the older generation of fifty-to-sixty-five-year-olds. Rather than have knowledge and information pushed at them by senior management, the context for this approach requires that young leaders be responsible for *pulling* experience and wisdom from the older generation. We always get more when we are committed to *getting what we need* rather than being told what we should know or how to think in a particular situation.

The process will begin by separately orienting the two generations to commit themselves to a different way of listening and learning. Learning in this context does not rely on classroom models or textbook answers. The process involves a shift in everyone's normal style of listening—from a top-down, hierarchical relationship to a more informal coaching relationship where the senior person guides the young leader to find his or her own answers.

Accelerated learning occurs within a structure that gives the younger generation responsibility for change management projects with very ambitious objectives normally owned by senior executives or outside experts. The projects must reflect real value and real work that needs to be done, must consider existing stress points and either replace current commitments or leverage work already being undertaken—they are not add-ons created for the sake of a learning objective. By working on very tough, even seemingly impossible objectives, the new managers and leaders get hands-on experience and the challenge of achieving breakthroughs in their leadership capabilities to succeed. This emphasis focuses everyone involved on acting in line with their commitments and the organization's need for change, possibly even reducing the requirement for additional staff or external resources.

This creates an atypically high standard for the developing leaders, requiring they demonstrate new, observable leadership qualities in a project structure before they will be called upon to demonstrate leadership in a broader organizational context. Both generations will focus on ensuring the developing leaders master a variety of "pre-distinguished" core qualitative competencies (ways of being) associated with mature leadership, including:

- Listening.
- Being "authentic"—committed communication.
- Engaging and empowering others.
- Innovating and creating possibilities.
- Making "unreasonable" requests.
- Assuming personal responsibility.
- Inspiring teams—creating alignment.
- "Walking the talk."
- Being held to account—holding others to account.
- Communicating vision and commitment.
- Creating and maintaining trust.
- Building powerful relationships and alliances.

- Taking a stand.
- Developing ethical sensibilities, integrity and humility.

While similar lists of "leadership competencies" have existed for years, they have always been regarded either as behaviors or as innate attributes of individuals (and therefore not seen as learnable). It is more useful to see these as learned aspects of who one is—ways of being that one develops over time as a leader. The critical questions are how long it takes and how we can acquire and manifest these qualities in the real world. With high project standards and a serious commitment on the part of the participants to the learning objectives, this approach to passing the torch offers the younger generation an opportunity to mature far beyond what would have normally been expected within the same time frame.

MULTI-DIMENSIONAL PAYOFF

Any organizational strategy to bring the next generation to a new level of authentic leadership should be designed to produce measurable results and to, at the very least, recover the costs of training, either through value-added results or enhanced efficiencies and productivity. This approach to accelerating leadership development can accomplish several important objectives at once:

- **Deliver outstanding results on real-world projects that reflect the vision and commitment of both today's and tomorrow's leaders.** Taking the top five recurring issues—those extremely ambitious challenges almost everyone accepts as important if something could be done about them—and giving them to the young (who will inherit them anyway) while lending them the full and unequivocal commitment of those who will be retiring opens the possibility for everyone to participate in manifesting a vision for the public service desperately desired by many in both generations.

- **Develop a more empowered, more prepared next generation of leaders**. Helping the next generation of leaders realize their full potential will have a direct impact on the results they achieve throughout their careers with the public service. When they and their predecessors can acknowledge, recognize, and appreciate each other's contributions toward their joint success, a positive organizational mood and culture will be created, one that impacts future recruiting (among other potentially positive outcomes).

- **Allow senior managers and executives to finish their careers with a genuine sense of having made a difference**. Leaving their best behind, in terms of participating in an extraordinary project and of having assisted younger colleagues to accomplish breakthroughs in their own learning (that would probably otherwise not have occurred) allows them to successfully pass the torch and retire with a deeper sense of completion and a stake in the future success of their organization.

- **Foster the kind of personal camaraderie that can transcend the event of retirement**. These strong alliances often occur when participating in a tough breakthrough project and may create an opportunity for alumni to become informal advisory resources after retirement, or to perform other voluntary roles in much the same way informal friendships between committed individuals have always served us.

CHOOSING THE FUTURE

The facts are clear. The collective knowledge, experience, wisdom, and cultural sensibilities of the boomer generation will be walking out the door in the next decade. There is next to nothing in place beyond standard succession planning and training tools to prepare the next generation to take the helm of governance. In the past, the numbers of people transitioning at any one time was relatively manageable—those who were still seasoned could easily assimilate changes in management and the next generation of leaders could be developed informally and naturally over time. The transfer of leadership from the boomers has begun, and the demographics are changing both the scale and potential impact of how the transfer of leadership is managed. Hopefully, the next generation will learn what they need to learn in time.

I see an opportunity to successfully transfer leadership and power by accelerating the learning of the next generation so they can be more confident, more prepared and more inspired than any "class" of leaders in the past. The public service can create an opening for those who will be retiring in the next five years or so to take on and accomplish what they've been saying needs to be done for years. In addition, we can give their successors the chance and the wherewithal to take on the most meaningful and difference-making challenges sooner rather than later. There is also the possibility of implementing a vision for the public service that has been talked about in various speeches and leadership initiatives for years.

The future is always a choice. The critical questions we always face are what future we will choose and who will be accountable for bringing it about. If we envision an organizational culture of authentic leadership and empowered individuals, then we now have a unique opportunity to co-create this future together. Passing the torch means giving today's and tomorrow's leaders a design where the younger generation takes responsibility and accountability for making this future reality before they have the authority to do so.

What future will we choose?

CHAPTER 8

RESPECT AND LEADERSHIP

Respect is one of the values that we hear talked about a lot in organizations. It is a word that always evokes a positive conversation—"yes, respect is very important, we value respect, and we need to be more respectful," and so forth. The problem is that almost no one really thinks about or understands what it means to respect someone, create a culture of respect among people, or for that matter what it means to be respected. Most of us believe that respect is an important value and that it is good. We do not normally think of respect as an action but as a feeling or judgment about other people.

To understand and distinguish respect, it is important to recognize that language is fundamental to how we see the world. Language both opens possibilities and empowers us, or it closes possibilities and limits us. For example, the word *respect* derives from the Latin word *respectus*, which means "to look" or "to look back." This word also brings to mind the notion of "spectacles," "spectator," and "spectacular." In other words we can distinguish the term as having something to do with "looking" or "observing." If we take the prefix *re* to imply "again," then we have the notion of respect as meaning something like "looking again."

If we say we respect someone, we are "looking" at the other person in a particular way—usually suggesting we are open to listen and honor each other's views even if we disagree. If we say we don't respect someone, we are generally closed to certain possibilities and conversations with them. Likewise, if we have "self-respect" we are generally in a healthy internal conversation with ourselves. If we don't respect ourselves, we will typically be stuck in all sorts of unproductive and unsatisfying "self-talk." If we say that something is possible to someone we respect, we will more than likely have a productive and satisfying dialogue. If we don't respect them then we will more than likely be closed, not listen, or in some cases disregard and dismiss them and their views outright.

Respect is just a word, but what it means and what it distinguishes for us can make all the difference in how we observe ourselves and others—as well as how we relate to future possibilities and choices. As mentioned, our conventional wisdom considers "respect" to be a kind of feeling, or more often than not a judgment of a person's "worthiness." But respect can also be a declaration on the part of one person who is respecting another. If we take this to be the case, then respect is something else altogether. While "respect" is always a context for relationship, we have a choice about whether it is created as an expression of our commitment to relating effectively with other human beings or whether it becomes part of a culture and worldview that separates and limits us.

Whether respect is declared or whether it occurs as a judgment, it is an expression of the way the person who is respecting or not respecting sees him- or herself and others. Respect is in the eye of the beholder and is not a function of the behavior or attributes of those we are relating to. Further, to understand respect as an empowering concept, it must also be universal. If respect is a judgment, it becomes a tool of the ego and actually a source of separation and conflict between human beings. The alternative is to understand that respect is an action, a declaration, and a commitment on our part to who another person is separate and apart from whatever judgments we might have of this person's behavior.

Finally, if we can create a culture in which respect is universal and an expression of our commitment to each other as human beings and how we choose to "look at each other," then we have a foundation for designing ways for collaboration and mutual empowerment that are simply not possible in the absence of authentic respect. Leaders are responsible for creating a culture of universal respect, and there are many ways to do this. I believe that respect is the foundation for any serious discourse on coaching, leadership, or building satisfying relationships with others. Without respect there are no possibilities for trust, sharing a vision, empowerment, or for creating powerful teams and organizations.

CONVENTIONAL WISDOM

Respect is one of the terms people often preach as a virtue but, in fact, can use as a weapon for manipulation and control of others. For example, how often do we hear someone say, "I don't feel respected" in a context of blaming others and demanding that "they" change? We hear people use "not feeling respected" as a justification for all sorts of counterproductive and even destructive behavior including being victims of their environment and prevailing systems of authority. Respect (or lack of it) is a core aspect of any recurring conflict situation as well as an integral factor in most labor-management disputes. Many times, we use the term and our feelings about respect to in effect say, "You should agree with me and behave the way I want you to or it means you don't respect me (or justifies my not respecting you) and therefore I can rationalize doing just about anything I want without concern for you."

Regardless of whether we think about respect as a judgment based on our feelings or view respect as a commitment or a declaration of "who another is for us" or "who we are for ourselves," respect is always in the eye of the beholder and it always becomes a context for relationship. For example, most of us will acknowledge that we have some list of negative assessments about ourselves and others—we think we (or they) are too lazy or not good-looking or not competent enough. When we believe our judgments are "truths," we objectify ourselves and others and generally conclude whether we (or they) are worthy of our respect. In an organizational or social context, our judgments and level of respect become the basis for how we relate to other people on a day-to-day basis.

In a personal and psychological context, self-judgments occur as "facts" and typically means that our "self-esteem" becomes hostage to whether we respect ourselves or not. Self-respect has exactly the same nature and character as our respect or lack of respect for others. In conversations with ourselves, we often find that we "know" about "the way we are" as if our assessments about ourselves are more "true" than other people's assessments of us. This condition of self-judgment inevitably becomes part of a closed worldview and can lead to all sorts of "self-referential" behavior and "self-justification," which upon close examination reveals an objectification of the "way we are" and resignation that change is unlikely at best. Since most of us don't claim perfection this means that we become trapped in an interpretation of self in which something about the way we are isn't OK, and we can't change it because our life experience has provided the experiential proof that we are the way we think we are. The result is we don't respect ourselves because we aren't OK the way we are and we can't (or haven't been) successful in changing ourselves. Many people live large portions of their lives suffering in a closed "internal conversation" about the way they, others, and life "should be" without ever realizing that they are living in a state of disrespect for themselves, for life, and for others.

That respect is fundamental to human relationships (and relationship with self) is not a new idea. What is new is the inquiry into whether it is possible to respect people with whom we strongly disagree and whose actions and behavior are inconsistent with what we value. We all use respect (or lack of respect) to determine how open we are, how trusting we are, and how we choose to relate to others. For example, in growing up with my children, I have lived with a lot of the younger generation's behavior, which was inconsistent, foreign, and even threatening to my own values and standards. Some of these behaviors included brightly colored hair, frequent use of strong scatological language, tattoos, and body piercing. If I add to this an exceptionally open and casual attitude toward sex on the part of many young people and lots of experimentation with drugs and alcohol, then the list of "negative assessments" begins to be significant. Can I respect people who behave in these ways, even if they are my own children?

I am not arguing intergenerational differences here, I am suggesting that if we think about it, there are many people (in every generation) who behave (for whatever reasons) in ways that push or exceed the limits of our own view of what is and what is not acceptable. When we have negative judgments, our assessments become the justification to not give respect. In our everyday way of relating, we rarely notice that the judgments and assessments are one thing, and the conclusions and actions that follow are something else. We blur this distinction and forget that respect is always and only something in the eye of the beholder and is never "caused" by those we respect or don't respect.

Therefore, to create a culture in which people naturally and authentically respect each other, we need to consider how we are looking at people already. That is, we need to observe that we are normally judging others in terms of our own values and practices. Our baseline for assessing others is essentially what we happen to believe at a given moment. The implication of this has to do with whether we can take someone seriously if they don't meet or match our standards and beliefs. If we can't take someone seriously then we never have the conversations that could make a difference in how we relate or what is or isn't possible for us in the future. When this occurs we become trapped in a vicious cycle of judgment/lack of respect/reaction, and more judgment that justifies more lack of respect.

It is, of course, possible to partially finesse the issue by trying to separate the "human being" from the behavior: "I respect *you*, but don't respect your behavior." This does distinguish and separate domain of "self" from "behavior" and does leave the individual whole, but is still based on having a superior judgment of which behaviors are worthy and which ones are not. Therefore it is still a way of using respect in order to maintain some degree of control over the other's behavior. While separating "self" from behavior is more responsible than simply writing off the whole human being as "unworthy," it is still a trap that ultimately will undermine relationships, weaken practices for coordination, and destroy any possibility of breakthroughs.

RESPECT EVERYONE?

We can't talk about respect for very long before we consider the "who" it is that is being respected or is not respected. I am suggesting that we must respect everyone if the idea of respect is to make any sense other than as a tool for judging and manipulating behavior. The reason for this is that the simple act of judging whether someone (including ourselves) is worthy of our respect is to separate ourselves from the other person as a human being and assume a "superior" relationship to them. To pass judgment from a position of superiority is in effect not seeing someone as having equal value, choice, and responsibility for his or her actions. To judge another as worthy or unworthy is itself an act of disrespect. In this context we are using the notion of respect as a weapon for control and domination—saying, "I approve (or disapprove) of you and what you are doing" as if we were the judge and in doing so implying that "if you want my respect you must behave consistent with my standards—otherwise you are unworthy."

If we don't respect everyone then we can respect no one, including ourselves. As a judgment, respect is used by the ego as a means for remaining separate and apart from others. This can also form the foundation for justifying perpetuating conflict between human beings. The alternative is to understand that respect is an action, a declaration, and a commitment on our part of who another person is separate and apart from whatever judgments we might have of their behavior. This means that we do not sacrifice the background of relationship over our differences and disagreements. This is crucial since relationship is the foundation for any sort of collaborative enterprise whether it is a nation, multinational corporation, team, or a marriage. As long as our relationships are intact, we have room to negotiate and design new ways of working together or even in some cases to not work together—but as a choice and not a reaction.

If respect means to "look again," then the question is what are we looking for? We can look at someone to garner evidence of our preconceptions, stereotypes, and prejudices, or we can look for who they are as a possibility. As a coach, for example, I am always relating to people in two domains. One is who I say they are as a possibility; the other is who they are in a context of my judgments and their history. My choice is in which context I will relate to them. If I relate to another in a context of possibility then our work together is about their commitments, creating breakthroughs, and producing unprecedented results. If I relate to them in a context of their past and my assessments then the game typically becomes about me analyzing their behavior and attempting to "fix" or control them.

Respecting everyone is a stand we can take. It is not reasonable and it is not based on people's past behavior—it is "looking at people newly" as possibilities and as perfect in the context of their own lives. If we make this shift, then we still have issues and differences, but we no longer give or withhold ourselves and our respect as a condition of the other person's compliance with our point of view.

CREATING A CULTURE OF RESPECT

There are many ways to define culture. One way to see culture is that it is constituted by the everyday conversations people have about "the way it is around here." We can observe culture most directly by listening to the "hallway" conversations" in which people speak straight about what they think and "the way it really is" for them. There are several reasons why this view is both powerful and useful. First it allows us to create or change culture by simply changing our conversations and committing ourselves to new interpretations of "reality." Secondly, it opens a perspective in which every individual can be personally responsible for the culture and participate in its persistence or change through how we speak and listen in each and every conversation every day. Finally, observing culture as conversation makes values such as respect "actionable" since from this perspective words and commitments are actions in language. Our conversations can literally transform how we observe our environment, open new possibilities, and allow us to see choices we might not otherwise observe.

Creating a culture of respect begins with a commitment to seeing everyone as worthy of respect. We have already noted that while we don't always have a choice about our automatic judgments and predispositions, we do have a choice about what our assessments mean and the weight we give to them in our day-to-day relationships.

I want to emphasize that I am not proposing some sort of Pollyanna positive thinking about people. I am not suggesting that we somehow try to rationalize some sort of positive virtue in people that we otherwise don't respect. What I am proposing is that, as a practical matter, not respecting others costs each of us a great deal and contributes to the persistence of cultural practices that we say we don't want. If people are serious about

115

creating a future that has larger possibilities for everyone, then it begins with creating a different cultural reality in which we universally respect each other.

Another aspect of creating a culture of respect is to observe how the absence of whatever we say we value occurs on a day-to-day basis. For example, when we are not respecting someone or we don't feel respected, does this occur as a breakdown for us? Is it a call to action? Does it produce new conversations to align and strengthen relationship, clarify different views, and build greater confidence and trust? In a culture of respect there will be more straight talk (especially of negative assessments) because we respect each other. In a culture of respect, all sorts of relationship issues, differences, and lack of alignment become positive forces for change, not justifications for the status quo.

Obviously, one thing that would have to change is that we would need to "see the other persons newly"…we would need to look again, look past our judgments, and generate an interpretation of who that person is that would allow us to authentically respect them. We would need to become the source of respect as our context for relating and assume responsibility for whatever negative assessments we might have that would normally justify our lack of respect.

CONCLUSION

Human beings will always have judgments about themselves and others. It doesn't matter whether our judgments are positive or negative since no judgment is ever true or false anyway, no matter how many may agree or disagree with it. However, we have a choice about what we conclude from our assessments and the secondary meanings we give to them. If our judgments of each other are negative and we conclude that therefore the other is not worthy of our respect or that we therefore don't need to take each other seriously, then we are setting up an interpretation in which our actions are justified by assessments that were neither true or false in the first place. Further, we have created a context for our relationship in which "they" are responsible for our judgments and assessments. In effect we are setting up a structure of interpretation in which we are reacting to each other based upon what we are "observing" but are blind to the fact that our observations have more to do with us and the "meaning" we give to what we observe than they do with the other person.

Respect is one of many values we seek to "enculturate" in our organizations. Like all values, it cannot be legislated or regulated into existence. It can be learned, it can be coached, and it can be demonstrated by leaders everywhere. In the final analysis, respect is part of our "way of being" in the world and is a product of both our commitment and our everyday practices. Respect as we have distinguished it here is a context for all relationships and can be created through commitment in our everyday conversations. It is not reasonable, nor does it happen naturally. It is a conscious expression of who we are, who we aspire to be, and who we declare others are for us. Creating a culture of respect doesn't solve problems or predict any particular behavior. It does, however, shift the context, our consciousness, and the organizational paradigm in such a way that we need not sacrifice our relationships in moments of conflict and fear. Moreover, when we respect others, we are able to consider our own responsibility for our disagreements and differences, and most of all we can engage in dialogues to create a future in which everyone is included without perpetuating reactive cycles of distrust, resentment, and acrimony.

CHAPTER 9

ELDERING: MIDLIFE LEADERSHIP

I have distinguished leadership as a "way of being." Consequently the actions of a leader can manifest in a wide variety of contexts and situations. For example, there are exceptional managers whose effectiveness can be viewed as expressions of leadership. I have repeatedly said that leaders and coaches are virtually identical in terms of how they relate to the world and the distinctions they embody that enables them to make the difference in "creating" reality. Examples of leadership can be found in virtually any field, from the arts to business to science.

One can engage in a legitimate and usually productive inquiry into how leadership occurs from any perspective. For example, a number of years ago a group of women I worked with created a project to explore the differences between how leadership occurs for women. Their view was that most of the models and behaviors normally associated with leadership are historically "masculine." At the end of the day their questions led to a breakthrough (at least for the participants) in how they experienced and expressed themselves as leaders.

When we think of leadership as a context as distinct from particular behaviors or attributes or accomplishments, it becomes apparent that the "essential" aspects of leadership have to do with one's "way of being"—being responsible, having integrity, authenticity, courage, clarity, and so forth. It is this qualitative aspect of ourselves that has traditionally been thought to be something we are born with as distinct from something that can be learned and/or transferred to others. Most people still believe that leadership is something that is innate to the individual and is a kind of natural gift.

Many regard apprenticeship to be the best and perhaps the only way for learning and mastering these kinds of qualities or virtues.

Contexts or "ways of being" are fundamental phenomena of life—they are the openings for our conscious awareness, our thinking/perception, what is possible and not possible, and ultimately our choices and actions. These phenomena are created. They exist only as linguistic distinctions and in our declarations of reality and possibility. When viewed as commitments, they can be changed. "Being" becomes a domain of action. If a younger person wishes to acquire some wisdom from an older person, for example, what is really required is for them to embody the distinctions and commitments that the older person has mastered over time and make them their own. This is a distinct domain of learning independent of whatever skills or competencies are available in the new context.

WHY ELDERING?

Previously, in "Passing the Torch: Leadership in Transition," I spoke of how we can approach the transfer of leadership qualities from one generation to another. This is particularly important as more and more senior people are retiring and younger employees are being challenged to assume more and more responsibilities with less and less preparation. This points to a larger question of how any older or more experienced person can approach transferring what they've learned and mastered in life to those that follow. In effect, how do we share our "wisdom" with others?

Historically, this is the role of the elders. I am using the word *eldering* to distinguish this process—the process of transferring the best of our qualities and what we've learned and experienced to others such that it brings out the best in them. This is akin to midlife leadership.

We human beings face countless challenges. No single generation has the answers or the responsibility for the future. But we all have something to contribute. When we look at our concerns together, we can discover how the ways we interpret the world can either keep us stuck or empower us. We can see that we are interdependent and that we have choices (even when none seem to exist). We can begin to transform our challenges into opportunities to reinvent our world and ourselves.

To define eldering further, consider these concepts:

ELDERING IS SHARING PERSPECTIVES.

Breakthroughs and innovative solutions often appear when we are able to see things differently. Every generation grows up with a common history, a shared set of cultural stories, events, and expectations. As we age, experience and maturity can allow us to see our relationships with ourselves, other people, our circumstances, and time differently. To create a world that works for all of us, everyone needs to openly share their collective insights and perspectives with each other. New understanding and possibilities appear when we can see the world through each other's eyes.

ELDERING IS CREATING POSSIBILITIES WHERE NONE EXIST.

Many people make commitments to take on the seemingly intractable problems of the world. When we are eldering, we are also committing to creating a future that, if we were to rely on traditional thinking and history, seems impossible. Possibilities are, by definition, not "reality." If they were, they would be examples. Instead of finding "solutions" to "problems," we create possible futures to live into.

ELDERING IS COMMITTING TO EACH OTHER AND A COMMON FUTURE.

Eldering calls us to actively develop committed, mutually empowering relationships with people from all generations. We share the best of who we are. To co-create a future that isn't predictable, we commit to having focused, purposeful conversations that matter. Like coaches, we focus on developing and empowering individuals and teams who are "in action."

Eldering is "wisdom in action."™

We are willing to apply our collective wisdom and act in unprecedented, unreasonable, and what may seem to be counterintuitive ways. We see wisdom in making our vision of a world that works for everyone real. Rather than accomplishing this by controlling, manipulating, or resisting, we accept "what is" and enroll others in the possibilities we see.

ELDERING HISTORY

In the past, the word *eldering* meant handing down religious teachings or cultural traditions from one generation to the next. The elders were society's caretakers. They took care of the spiritual aspects or the collective knowledge and wisdom of the group. Younger generations looked to them for answers to their problems.

Eldering in the twenty-first century is not about age and experience presuming to have the answers for younger generations. The traditions and teachings of the past may no longer be relevant or valid in our rapidly changing world. I see eldering today as a collective, multigenerational movement to empower each other and transform the paradigms that limit what is possible for the future.

ELDERING: A COLLECTIVE AWAKENING

It is more crucial today than ever that the generations know and understand each other. When the young and old feel their differences are so immense that they can't communicate, the dialogue between the past and future—a dialogue that is essential to a humane and civilized world—is cut off.
—*Maggie Kuhn, founder of the Gray Panthers*

For the past three decades, the baby boomers have dominated the larger conversations and practices of the developed world. The boomers have had many experiences that changed the world, including mobilizing millions to participate in civil rights movements, world peace, equality, and antinuclear initiatives. But today's seemingly intractable problems—terrorism, resource depletion, global warming, and pandemics, to name a few—pose unprecedented challenges to our existing political, social, and economic structures.

The fact is no one—neither old nor young—knows what the "right" answers are to the problems we face today or the problems we will face tomorrow.

Now, for the first time in human history, more than half of us are going to be over fifty years of age. This demographic shift will influence our reality in profound and lasting ways. Just as the baby boomers shaped America's love affair with suburbia when we were toddlers and then brought us rock and roll and the Age of Aquarius as we grew up, our future will be shaped by the conversation of older boomers. What's at stake is whether that conversation will be about resigning ourselves to becoming spectators of our world or whether it will be a conversation for expanding possibility and participation.

Before we create new policies, laws, or enterprises, we must confront and resolve the larger question of whom we are choosing to be in relationship to "what is." The most important factor shaping that choice is designing the paradigm that defines our "reality."

CHANGING PARADIGMS

A paradigm is a prevailing and shared interpretation of the world—a collective worldview, if you will. It organizes how our "reality" occurs for us, determines what we see as being possible, and limits our choices. Our paradigm defines everything. For all practical purposes, our paradigms are our reality.

Each generation shares common experiences, history, cultural developments, and challenges: they literally live in different paradigms. As the rate of change increases exponentially, we find ourselves defining a new generation every few years (when we used to every few decades). The paradigmatic "gap" between generations—and between young and old—widens accordingly.

REALITY: PROBLEM OR BREAKDOWN?

Again and again in history some special people in the crowd wake up. They have no ground in the crowd, and they emerge according to much broader laws. They carry strange customs with them, and demand room for bold actions. The future speaks ruthlessly through them. They save the world.

—*Rainer Maria Rilke (1899)*

Our current paradigms persist because they are based in a belief that reality is a problem which human beings are destined to fix.

For most of us, anything that doesn't match our expectations, desires, or standards is viewed as a problem. Our solutions always result in more problems and greater complexity. Eventually, certain problems become intractable and we resign ourselves to believing that solutions are not possible.

So how to deal with intractable problems? What one person may consider being a viable solution (from the perspective of their generation's paradigm) may not be a solution at all for someone from another generation. We need an alternative way of observing the world. Consider that something is only a problem if we say it is. Our assessments define what is a problem and what is a solution. However, remember that assessments are only a statement of our perspective on the matter—they are neither true nor false.

Instead of focusing on problems that need fixing, we can identify anything that is obstructing or limiting us from achieving our commitments as a breakdown. For example, we may see global warming as a problem; however, if we are committed to living in a relatively stable, safe environment, personally experiencing the effects of climate change will occur as a breakdown for us. When we declare something is a breakdown, we escape the problem/solution mindset. We empower ourselves to take unprecedented actions to break through and create a new reality. We have the freedom to invent new structures and processes that combine the best of multiple paradigms. We are no longer victims of our circumstances.

THE FUTURE

It does not matter whether we are optimistic or pessimistic about the future. Optimism and pessimism are only different perspectives. Neither affects what the future will be.

The future will be a product of our individual and collective actions. The question is what will organize and determine our actions?. Problems and solutions, or breakdowns and breakthroughs?.

We are at a turning point in human history. We will either invent and implement a sustainable way of living in harmony or we will, in all likelihood, face a period of unprecedented suffering. This is the leadership challenge for our generation and those of our children and grandchildren. This is the challenge of eldering.

PART II

ORGANIZATIONAL TRANSFORMATION

INTRODUCTION INNOVATIONS IN THEORY AND PRACTICE

by Jim Selman, Suzanne DiBianca-Lieser and Sam Kirschner

Organizational leaders are perplexed and worn out by the *persistent* and *dynamic* jolts in today's business environment. "Rarely does a day go by," bemoans a company vice president, "that I don't feel the impact of yet another attack on my strategic direction." Any business leader can cite example after example of dramatic changes occurring in the world:

- Deregulation and privatization open markets.
- Breakthrough technology creates new industry leaders overnight.
- Court challenges drain companies of time and money.
- Mergers and acquisitions require immediate operating model changes.
- Large-scale restructuring efforts and layoffs lead to disgruntled employees and strikes.

Leaders know they can neither ignore these challenges nor let them dictate their organizational strategy. It is a classic Catch-22. Ignoring these challenges will ultimately result in erosion of market share, margin, stock price, and possibly the death of the company. Alternatively, allowing the changes to control a company's strategic direction would lead to a constant game of catch-up, frustration, cynicism, and eventually, apathy.

As a result of this constant flux in the corporate operating environment, many previously fundamental aspects of organizational life have become impediments to change:

- Rigid organizational structures, which once provided stability and control, are now political encumbrances that slow reaction time.
- Long-range plans gather dust as technology continues to rapidly reconfigure the competitive environment.
- Command and control leadership styles that once provided certainty have created internal competition between leaders, and a workforce that has no confidence anyone will listen to their ideas.
- Functional organizations that have deep, specialized knowledge are being subjugated by integrated organizations that offer a wide range of comprehensive services.
- Traditional operating models and long-standing vendor relationships are being threatened by the movement towards outsourcing both peripheral and core businesses.

As the ability to predict what will happen in the business environment has become virtually impossible, a company's ability to change, reinvent, and quickly reconfigure itself has become a competitive advantage. Prospering in this time of permanent unpredictability requires new ways of thinking and behaving. The scale and scope of these changes demands a *transformational process* in which the company designs not only new organizational operating models, strategies, and business processes, but also, more importantly, new competencies and practices. On a practical level, real agility in these times requires that an organization's members learn new tools that will allow them to react and respond to these challenges with possibility and creativity.

As the ability to predict what will happen in the business environment has become virtually impossible, a company's ability to change, reinvent, and quickly reconfigure itself has become a competitive advantage.

This section offers a transformational approach to managing change, an approach that enables all employees to become new observers and actors in their organization. In chapter 10, we will look at three major trends that have been permeating the contemporary business world and discuss their impact on the state of organizations today. Next, we will discuss two distinct strategic approaches that have emerged in response to "managing change." Finally, we will put forth an alternative approach to transforming organizations that *includes* the two approaches but is not limited by either one. Specifically, chapter 11 will describe the theoretical components that support the transformational approach and offer some enabling competencies for being effective in the domain of context. Chapter 12, the practice section, offers a detailed process, consisting of seven components, for bringing this approach into organizations. The practice section also provides some examples of both behavioral and practical business results we have seen in companies who have used this approach.

CHAPTER 10

ORGANIZATIONAL TRANSFORMATION BACKGROUND

TRENDS IN TODAY'S BUSINESS ENVIRONMENT

The importance of developing both theory and practice for creating a new strategic approach to managing change increases when we observe the trends of today's business environment. These trends have formed somewhat of a ritual mantra for business executives when talking about change. I have captured them in three general categories:

1. ORGANIZATIONS ARE DYNAMIC NETWORKS OF RELATIONSHIPS.

Over the past decade there has been a growing awareness inside of organizations that they are fluid networks of relationships and self-organizing systems rather than static, self-contained entities. The plethora of books and articles on the "ecology" of organizations demonstrates this view, as does the recent eruption of mergers and acquisitions, hostile takeovers, strategic alliances and the emergence of leading-edge technology partnerships. In one alliance, competitors are working side-by-side to develop new organizational operating models for a client. In another, we see CEOs of Fortune 500 companies working with directors of local community agencies and headhunters to create centers for employee recruiting and training.

As is most often the case, the shift in business has been closely paralleled with a shift in scientific discourse. Neurologists, physicists, biologists, and psychologists are all struggling with questions like "how do billions of interconnected cells in the brain give rise to awareness, cognition and feeling";[6] and "how do simple particles organize themselves into complex structures such as stars, snowflakes and hurricanes?"[7]

Instead of directing the focus on the quest for the ultimate particle, both science and business have been moving toward studies and practices concerned with flux, change and the forming and dissolving of patterns.

---

6   Waldrop, M. *The Emerging Science at the Edge of Order and Chaos.* New York: Touchstone, 1992.

7   Kauffman, S. *At Home in the Universe: The Search for the Laws of Self-Organization and Complexity.* New York: Oxford University Press, 1995. McMaster, M. *The Intelligence Advantage: Organizing for Complexity.* Douglas, UK: Knowledge Based Development Co. Ltd. 1995. Wheatley, M. and M. Kellner Rogers. *A Simpler Way.* San Francisco: Berrett-Koehler, 1996.

...both science and business have been moving toward studies and practices concerned with flux, change and the forming and dissolving of patterns.

The "quality" movement of the seventies and eighties—based largely on the design and control of distinct components in a process—grew into the more dynamic reengineering movement of the early nineties. This quantum shift began to, and continues to, move the focus toward understanding and redesigning networks and systems. What has often been overlooked in this process, however, is an intentional focus on the individual's role in taking accountability for the success of these networks of relationships and processes. The concept of self-organizing systems contains the assumption that people will *naturally* self-organize. Managers have unfortunately relied on this premise and have developed a sense of complacency because they think they don't have to *do* anything except massage the process. What is missing is an intentional focus on whether the system is organizing in a way that aligns with the company's *and* the individual's goals. Structures and processes need to be designed intentionally to allow people to be accountable for making these networks of relationships work.[8]

2. THE "GLOBALIZATION" OF BUSINESSES AND MARKETS CONTINUES TO GROW.

Industry lines have been blurred, local markets have expanded, and the "democratization" of countries—particularly in Asia, Latin America, and Europe—have dramatically changed the

---

8   Fritz, R. *Corporate Tides.* San Francisco: Berrett-Koehler, 1996.

Mohrmann, S.A., Cohen, S.G., and A.M. Mohrmann, Jr. *Designing Team Based Organizations.* San Francisco: Jossey Bass, 1995.

Stacey, R. *Complexity and Creativity in Organizations.* San Francisco: Berrett-Koehler, 1996.

nature of our global marketplace. The massive investment in infrastructure and business-process redesign resulting from globalization demands some universal interpretation of human action and coordination that transcends cultural differences. In this environment, organizations must acknowledge not only linguistic and cultural disparities, but also must take into account local technological capability, variable economic conditions, and educational inequalities. An organization's members see the world from different points of view and value systems, and in response, companies have attempted to establish a "common ground" on which to conduct business.

The creation of a common ground—although built on good intentions—has often led to the homogenization of corporate operating environments. In other words, many organizations have not embraced these differences, they have tried to conquer them. The "melting pot" mentality is pervasive in organizations when dealing with issues of diversity: it minimizes and blends differences rather than enhances them, like a mosaic would. Instead of seeing how each individual can make a distinct contribution, some organizations have put people in cross-functional teams and blended their expertise, making the team accountable for the results. In some situations this has proven effective, but in the majority of cases when a person can blame the team for his/her mistakes, personal ownership is lost, and the success of the team is diminished.

Furthermore, the shift to free market structures around the globe has dramatically changed the nature of security for employees. Put simply, the locus of security has changed. As markets and industries have evolved and grown, competition has increased, and companies have had to "streamline" to keep costs down and margins high. Employees' sense of responsibility for the enterprise has been replaced by the question, "Will I be out of a job tomorrow?" No longer can employees rely on their companies to provide security; instead they must generate a sense of security from within. People need to develop the capabilities and resourcefulness that will provide them with internal satisfaction and accomplishment, regardless of the circumstance. It is this dramatic shift from an institutional form of security to developing employees' internal sense of security that leads us to stressing the importance of personal transformation as an access to changing an organization's culture.

Employees' sense of responsibility for the enterprise has been replaced by the question, "Will I be out of a job tomorrow?"

3. TECHNOLOGICAL ADVANCES ARE CHANGING THE WAY ORGANIZATIONS CHANGE.

Technology is driving the rate of change. The intensifying spiral of upgrades and breakthroughs in technology are forcing competitors to rapidly match each other's improvements. Federal Express, for example, developed an electronic package-tracking system to expedite customer queries, and within a month the United Postal Services (UPS) developed a package-tracking system that surpasses that of FedEx, both in terms of technological competence and price. Technology requires that not only organizations, but also individuals, constantly assess and upgrade their skills and capabilities as their organizations change.

Moreover, technology has become inexorably linked with every other aspect of the business model. We can't even think about strategy or any other organizational process without considering both the implications and opportunities that technology provides. The convergence of strategy, technology, and process has created the need for an organization to look towards changing and reinventing itself on a regular basis. Technology has truly made change the status quo for organizations today. A recent article on managing change states, "Change is the business environment. And it's not that every company is undergoing change. Change has taken over every company. Creating change, managing it, mastering it, and surviving it is the agenda for anyone in business who wants to make a difference."[9] Technology, and our relationship to it, is a key lever for an organization's ability to prosper in these times of constant change.

Creating change, managing it, mastering it, and surviving it is the agenda for anyone in business who wants to make a difference.
—C. Fishman, The Ten Laws of Change That Never Change

Technology is further disrupting what used to be relatively stable businesses and industries. Technological breakthroughs have become normal in almost every field. Like globalization, this has perpetuated the race to operate as lean and mean as possible in order to stay on the leading edge of technological advances. Because companies are unfamiliar with this continual demand for shedding expenses and layers, instead of becoming more vibrant, these efforts have often left organizations in an anorexic condition. People are tired, disoriented, anxious, and cynical about their future. They are looking for certainty in an uncertain world.[10] Without a deliberate effort to incorporate people and provide them with new skills and some direct accountability for the company's success (as well as

9   Fishman, C. "The 10 Laws of Change That Never Change" *Fast Company Magazine*, 1997 (8).

10   Handy, C. *Beyond Uncertainty*. Boston, MA: HBS Press, 1996.

their own) the logical end of this game turns into washed out margins and a burned-out work force.

IMPLICATIONS FOR THE FUTURE OF ORGANIZATIONS

How can an organization prosper and grow in this state of permanent unpredictability? The answer lies in the ability of both the organization and its work force to fundamentally alter their relationships with themselves, each other, emerging technologies, and the business environment in which they operate. This change will require flexible and efficient coordination of capabilities and an ability to build, modify, and sustain relationships with both partners *and* competitors.[11] Financial services, health care, insurance, and management consulting are just a few examples of industries that are facing demands from their clients to offer "integrated" capabilities and services at an accelerated pace.

The ability to respond, expand, and innovate no longer depends simply on how smart or savvy we are but, in addition, depends on how quickly we can adapt to the changing marketplace. The transformational approach claims that organizations can build specific organizational competencies and practices that will produce freedom, power, possibility, and choice *regardless* of the situation or circumstance. These competencies will rely on two pertinent capabilities: the ability to consistently and accurately sense conditions and know when it is time to reinvent the organization; and a willingness to embrace being in a state of constant personal and organizational transformation.

---

11   Goldman, S.L., Nagel, R.N., and K. Preiss. *Agile Competitors and Virtual Organizations.* New York: Van Nostrand Reinhold, 1995.

PREVAILING WISDOM FOR CHANGE MANAGEMENT

Over the past twenty-five years, two broad approaches for transforming organizations have emerged: "cultural initiatives" and "strategic and structural initiatives" (see Figure A). Neither approach has shown to be sufficient in the long term. The best attempts at creating organizations that can be flexible and resilient in the face of change are those that intend to bridge both approaches.[12] Even these attempts have had minimal success.

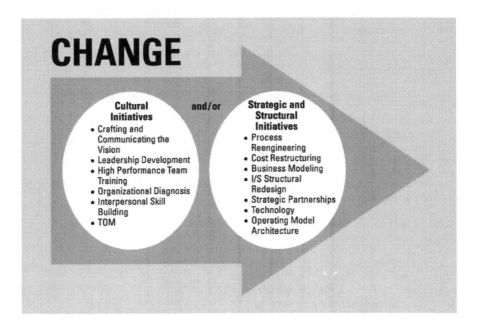

Figure A: Examples of Traditional Approaches to Managing Change

"CULTURAL" INITIATIVES

In their 1982 best seller, *In Search of Excellence*, Tom Peters and Robert Waterman recognized and articulated the importance

12   Champy, J. *Reengineering Management.* New York: Harper Business, 1995.

of having a strong corporate culture. The authors argued that successful companies altered their cultures by first assessing the dysfunctional dynamics of the organization and then mobilizing employees to act in new ways. Although many companies in this book have since faltered, the importance of cultural initiatives remains in tact. The cultural strategy may include an organizational diagnosis with feedback, team building, diversity training, and other well-established interpersonal skill-building interventions.

Research has shown that, although attitudes and behaviors are often altered in the short term, long-lasting organizational change cannot occur without accompanying substantive structural and systemic changes.[13] For example, many organizations that have shifted to "team based" work structures that have not made adequate changes in their information technology systems, reporting structures, or human resource policies have been unable to sustain this new work model.[14] Some of these companies have abandoned the team approach all together and are now looking to *alternatively* redesign their processes to create results and increase productivity.

Another theory as to why cultural initiatives are not sustainable in the long run is that organizations are a reflection of human nature. There is, it is argued, an initial inertia that an organization needs to overcome in order to get the change started; and once this happens the organization often thinks that it is "done." However, similar to human nature, these change efforts erode over time if the organization does not *consistently and intentionally* regenerate them. Staying on a diet, for example, is more difficult than starting one. Therefore, sustaining the new state is actually

---

13   Beer, M. and E. Walton, "Developing the Competitive Organization; Interventions and Strategies," *American Psychologist*, 1990, 45.

14   Mohrmann, S.A., Cohen, S.G., and A.M. Mohrmann, Jr. *Designing Team Based Organizations*. San Francisco: Jossey Bass, 1995.

more difficult than creating it, because continual change requires even more energy and commitment than the initial investment. Throughout the change process, management needs to ensure that it is continually stopping, evaluating, and reinvesting the required resources and energy necessary to see its efforts come to fruition. Only through a consistent evaluation and regeneration process can the organization move to the next level of change.

"STRATEGIC AND STRUCTURAL" INITIATIVES

The strategic and structural approach has been shown to be highly effective in reducing costs and streamlining organizations in the short term. This approach has taken various forms: process reengineering, cost restructuring, strategic planning, business modeling, compensation system overhaul, or redesigning the work architecture. Although the specific techniques and methodologies are very different under each, the primary goal is the same: cost reduction, revenue optimization, and an increase in the quality of products or services.

These efforts have often produced the intended results in the long term because many companies "confuse mechanical rearrangement of work processes and systems for holistic transformation and turn it into a *strategy* which leads to an ignominious death."[15] Strategic and structural work by itself can prove intimidating, dehumanizing, and disempowering to the employee network based on negative associations and beliefs. These negative associations are not surprising, as downsizing and layoffs have often been masked as "corporate restructuring" programs. Research has shown that even when a company tries to reconfigure their work model by creating an Employee Stock Ownership Program (ESOP) or some other type of increased productivity incentive, the effort often

---

15   Gouillart, F. and Kelly J. *Transforming the Organization*. New York: McGraw-Hill, 1995.

fails to produce the intended results because there is no cultural component to teach people new ways to communicate and act.[16]

In the nineties we witnessed an emergence of enterprise-wide technology solutions (e.g., SAP) that link business processes in a more integrated way. These solutions *are* moving in the right direction as the intention is to unite the whole enterprise in a cohesive and consistent way. Nevertheless, these solutions are merely another example of an engineer's approach to consolidating an organization without accounting for the human factor, other than seeing people solely as the medium to get the work done. What they are learning is much the same as the lessons learned in reengineering; namely, if the company views the process exclusively as an engineering one, they will be limited both in their thinking and their success.

THE ORGANIZATIONAL DOUBLE BIND

The two prevailing strategies are more than differences in style or preference; they are inherently juxtaposed to one another. The underlying logic of the cultural orientation is *that people are senior to processes and systems*, and ultimately, are free agents responsible for their actions. The underlying logic of the strategic and structural orientation is *that processes and structure don't merely influence human behavior, they define and control it.* Essentially, these two models are held in an either/or relationship. To simply declare that both are equally important cannot produce an integrated outcome in practice, because it is not possible for an individual to simultaneously have choice and *not* have choice.[17] In effect, most organizations are in a double

16   Rosen C. and Quarrey M. "How Well Is Employee Ownership Working?" *Harvard Business Review*, September 1987.

17   Bateson, G. *Steps to an Ecology of Mind*. New York: Ballantine Books, 1972.

bind in which people are either empowered as responsible actors or objectified as functions within some predefined and procedurally constructed process.

Either people are in the service of the enterprise, or the enterprise is in the service of human commitments and concerns. If the context one chooses is that people are senior to processes, then strategies and initiatives will be put in place to support that based on what the people say they want. For instance, a manufacturing organization may choose process as the senior design component and subsequently work to empower people on the assembly line through training and educational sessions. An insurance company, on the other hand, may choose people as the senior component in design and set up self-managed work teams to redesign their claims and collection processes. A company can choose either context; neither is right or wrong, but it is important that the strategies that are put in place follow whatever design choice is selected.

Business leaders are traditionally uncomfortable making choices at this elemental level because it can appear superfluous to the work that needs to get done. Failure to do so, however, typically will lead to practices and actions based on the past—particularly in relationship to politics and power. Integrating both dimensions of change is both possible and relatively straightforward when organizations recognize that they have choice at every moment and in every circumstance. This view has been beautifully expressed in an Edwin Markham poem: "*They drew a circle to keep me out, with anger, fury and clout. But love and I decided to win, so we drew a circle to keep them in.*" In essence, our transformational approach does this at the onset, by disclosing the fact that a contextual design choice needs to be made for setup and implementation to go smoothly.

AN ALTERNATIVE—THE "TRANSFORMATIONAL" STRATEGY

The transformational approach is a new model that incorporates strategy, human relationships, practices for coordination, work structures and processes, information systems, and technology into an integrated "whole" (see Figure B).

Figure B: The Transformational Approach to Managing Change

In addition, this approach includes working with companies in developing and transferring what we call "enabling competencies." Enabling competencies are those practices that help people be effective in managing in the domain of context, and are capabilities that develop overtime, based on the commitment of the organization to operate in a new way.

One of the primary benefits that the transformational approach affords is the ability to work on issues in the background that often go unnoticed or unstated, but are nevertheless critical to having the change effort succeed. Behind every action that a person takes is a commitment that often goes unnoticed. When we are assisted in identifying this "background commitment" a wider range of choice is available. A background commitment can most easily be demonstrated through a simple, yet poignant example: A mother starts yelling at her husband because he hasn't buckled their baby's seat belt. The baby's father (being tuned into this notion of background commitment) sees that what is in the background of his wife's concern is the child's safety. Instead of yelling back at her, he can choose to react to her in a different way. That is, he can directly communicate with her in a way that acknowledges her concern for their child and asserts his mutual commitment.

In a business setting we can explore another example: HR practitioners make decisions and take actions based on their own assessments of what is needed to move a change effort forward. They may suggest changing compensation structures in accordance with the redesign of a particular department. I/T professionals, on the other hand, make different decisions according to their own assessments of what is needed to move forward. For instance, they may suggest that new information systems are required to support a new way of working. Both ideas originate in the historical interpretation of what the person believes to be relevant and true. Neither is right or wrong. The views are simply assessments based on individual knowledge and experience.

In the transformational approach we would be able to see that the HR practitioner who wants new compensation systems has a larger commitment (in the background), which goes something like, "I think it is important for our employees to feel valued." Similarly, the engineer may have his/her own background commitment, which may sound something like, "It is important to me that our employees have an easy and efficient way to communicate." These commitments are not so different, and if unearthed, will provide the basis for an integrated solution that is more powerful and sustainable in the long run. In this example, once the participants see what they have in common, they may decide to work together in creating a compensation system based on performance, made visible and simple by a new information system that tracks sales performance in each location.

This process also offers a unique ability to uncover historical interpretations and background commitments that often reside at a subconscious level of awareness. Moreover, it affords people the opportunity to examine where their assessments originate, providing a larger context for both to exist, while coordinating actions in a way that produces extraordinary results.

Finally, the transformational approach allows a company to experience itself more directly: getting the background commitments and conversations out on the table. Dealing with what is going on in the company in the present moment allows for distinguishing what implications that will have on their desired state.

The transformational strategy involves an empowering consultative relationship that provides the "high touch" component necessary to offset what is often perceived as the "high tech" disregard for the importance of the person.

CHAPTER 11

THEORETICAL UNDERPINNINGS OF THE TRANSFORMATIONAL APPROACH

ONTOLOGY AND CONTEXT

The transformational approach to managing change is grounded in part in the ontological and philosophical works of Martin Heidegger. The part of Heidegger's work this philosophy embraces basically says that human beings are never dealing with a "fixed" reality; rather they operate within a world which is a function of their past experiences.[18] This view allows people to see the world in terms of "interpretations" rather than immutable facts. People often fail to realize that what they believe to be true about themselves and the world is, for the most part, merely unconscious assessment that they labeled "right" in the past.

Ontology, one of the "first" philosophies along with the study of existence or *being*,[19] examines why people respond and react to similar situations in different ways. I believe that studying this philosophy is critical for building a sustainable capability for change because it allows us to inquire into the *nature* of context. Specifically, we examine ontology because it tells us about the general structures of our world. We can contrast these most general structures with the structures produced by other worldviews. In this way we may arrive at a deeper insight into our own worldviews.[20]

The transformational approach is based on a set of three ontological claims about the nature of human beings. These claims are central to understanding context, and encompass a theory of behavior, commitment, and organization.

ONTOLOGIC PROPOSITION
CLAIM 1—HUMAN BEHAVIOR IS A FUNCTION OF HOW WE VIEW THE WORLD.

Heidegger's work asserts that all behavior is a product of an underlying common "state" or interpretation of the world. Over the years, business leaders have labeled these states in

18   Heidegger, M. *Being and Time.* Translated by J. Macquarte and E. Robinson. New York: Harper & Row, 1968.

19   Winograd, T. and F. Flores. *Understanding Computers and Cognition: A New Foundation for Design.* Reading, MA: Addison-Wesley, 1987.

20   For more information on ontology we recommend the following publication:

Oppenheimer, P., and Zalta, E. "On the Logic of the Ontological Argument" in J. Tomberlin (ed.) *Philosophical Perspectives* 5: Ridgeview (1991): 509-29.

various ways: paradigms, logics, points of view, institutionalized metaphors, frames, interpretive schemes, worldviews, and deep structures.[21] The transformational approach believes that the nature of this underlying common state or "context" in which we view the world is constituted by:

- **Personal History.** People often fail to recognize the role of their past in shaping how they perceive reality and determine meaning from everyday occurrences. Our behavior and actions are *always* correlated with what we observe to have worked or not worked in the past. It is useful if you want to replicate behavior; however, it won't allow for anything new to emerge or any breakthroughs to occur.

- **Distinctions.** Competence in a particular domain begins with learning a new distinction. Distinctions are learned and "embodied" through practice. When a new distinction is mastered, it constitutes a transparent background for cognition and action, and behavior becomes automatic, spontaneous, and "natural." For example, there are certain professionals who have the distinction "group dynamics" and therefore have a whole set of terms, insights, and practices that other people may not have. They can assess

21   The following individuals are attributed with coining these terms in the business context:

Paradigms—Kuhn, T. *The Structure of Scientific Revolutions.* 2d ed. Chicago: University of Chicago Press, 1970.

Logics—Horn, R. *Trialectics: Toward a Practical Logic of Unity.* Lexington: Lexington Institute, 1983.

Points of View—Ford, J. and L. Ford. "The Role of Conversations in Producing Intentional Change in Organizations," *Academy of Management Review,* 1995, 20 (3).

Institutionalized Metaphors—Johnson, P. "Why I Race Against Phantom Competitors," *Harvard Business Review,* 1988.

Frames—Fairhurst, G. and R. Sarr. *The Art of Framing: Managing the Language of Leadership.* San Francisco: Jossey-Bass, 1996.

Interpretive Schemes—Ranson, Hinings, and Greenwood. "The Structuring of Organization Structures," *Administrative Science Quarterly,* 1978, 25.

Worldviews and Deep Structures—Lincoln, Y. *Organizational Theory and Inquiry: The Paradigm Revolution.* Beverly Hills: Sage, 1985.

a group's ability to work together, provide skills for resolving conflicts, and teach practices for acting as a high performance team. The more distinctions we have, the more choices for action we have.

CLAIM 2—HOW WE SEE THE WORLD IS A FUNCTION OF OUR COMMITMENTS.

A central tenet of this approach implies that human beings always have some choice about what happens in their world, and that choice, when consciously made and articulated, becomes a commitment.[22] Specifically,

- **Commitments are being generated and fulfilled (or not) constantly.** It is *not* possible to be uncommitted. For example, when a we say that we are not committed to (yet another) organizational change program, there is still something underneath to which we *are* committed. One possibility is that we are committed to doing some work that we feel will truly make a difference. Once we see that this is our background commitment, new choices are available, and perhaps we will choose to be involved in the change program in a way that *will* make a difference.

- **Commitment is what distinguishes one interpretation of reality from another.** Each person can easily generate at least two interpretations of the same situation. A classic example is the question "is the glass half full or half empty?" The issue isn't which is correct; it depends on our agenda. Do we want to quench our thirst, or do we want something to put flowers in?

- **Commitments become obligations when we fail to stop and reevaluate what is important for us.** This is most often

---

22 Winograd, T. and F. Flores. *Understanding Computers and Cognition: A New Foundation for Design.* Reading, MA: Addison-Wesley, 1987.

where we get "stuck" in life. Commitments must be regenerated constantly or they simply become memories that may, or may not, serve us anymore. Action based on memory is often routine and conceals choice in the present moment. When we take a new job, for example, we must regenerate our commitment to that job every day from then on, or it will become an obligation and eventually apathy and resignation will set in. Often people get stuck because they don't notice (or take action on) a commitment that has changed or needs to be regenerated.

- **The principal action of managers and leaders is making, keeping, sharing, evoking, and coordinating commitments.** Project management, strategic planning, and focusing on customer service are all forms of discerning and coordinating different commitments. The role of a manager, leader, or coach is principally to speak, listen, and act in ways that clarify, align, and coordinate commitments within complex networks of relationships.

CLAIM 3—ORGANIZATIONS ARE A NETWORK OF RELATIONSHIPS AND COMMITMENTS.

Organizations are comprised of relationships—networks of conversations and actions among individual human beings who are attempting to take care of each other's concerns. This is done by coordinating actions to accomplish something that can't be accomplished individually. When work is viewed this way (as a conversation leading to action), it gives us access to altering our situation by changing the conversation.

For example, one CEO I worked with was consistently viewed by his executive team as detached from the reality of the current business condition (which, at the time, had been slowly deteriorating). They complained to each other that he was in denial and suspected he was covering up critical information that would make him look bad. After some intense coaching, they confronted him as a team. Only then did they find out that what looked to them like denial and cover-up was really his way of fulfilling on his commitment to turn the company around. He had been spending the last month doing an unusually intensive assessment of an under-performing business unit that would eventually be spun off, ultimately leading to a sharp increase in stock price and margin. In essence, what this team did was take a risk and reveal their interpretations (which felt more like facts) and their personal commitments to the CEO. After a difficult but rewarding meeting, the conversation "he is detached" was replaced with "he is on top of our business and knows what he is doing." This not only empowered the CEO to make better decisions, but also empowered the team to stay in better communication with him.

In essence, these three claims create a context for the transformational approach, which is:

- Grounded in how people are being (their ontology).
- Based on distinguishing what their commitments are.
- Manifested in how they manage their relationships to themselves, their organizations, and each other.

While transformation may be accurately viewed as a continuous and never-ending process, a specific example of organizational transformation can be distinguished and declared complete when an observable or measurable outcome, previously judged to be unlikely to occur or impossible to attain, is being intentionally produced on a recurring basis. In one company, cycle time for a new product was cut in half, from eighteen months to nine months. This was a transformational result for them, as initially they said the most they could possibly reduce the time was 25 percent. Such changes *can* be achieved without creating a context of personal responsibility, but such dramatic changes cannot be *sustained*. They also cannot be regenerated in a different moment or circumstance, or experienced as an accomplishment, without personal responsibility. This is the primary difference between transformation as an event or solution, and transformation as a process of continual creation.

> *...changes* can *be achieved without creating a context of personal responsibility, but such dramatic changes cannot be* sustained.

UNDERSTANDING AND ACCESSING CONTEXT ENABLING COMPETENCIES

For an organization to be effective in the domain of context, new competencies and practices are needed. We offer these competencies as truly enablers for the seven-step process, as they are continually being taught and transferred throughout the duration of our work with companies. Both leaders and employees need to be as deliberate and confident in their capacity to work in the realm of context as they are in other, more familiar domains. To achieve this, one needs to pursue mastery in at least the following nine enabling competencies:

NINE ENABLING COMPETENCIES

1. Live in Accordance with Your Word

Many theories we come across in the field of change management represent people in terms of their qualities (e.g., trustworthy, impulsive) or by their specific characteristics (e.g., open-minded, soft-spoken). The ontological basis suggested by our approach implies that people are constituted not by their qualities or characteristics, but by history and language. There is not a "fixed" or absolute set of properties or attributes that add up to what a human being is. Rather, since we view people as malleable, we believe that they are capable of, and responsible for, defining and creating themselves and each other moment by moment. The definitions that are chosen begin with language, are a function of their commitments, manifest through the actions they take in the world, and can be modified or changed with intentional effort.

Living as one's word is a choice every human being is capable of, and once made, will alter one's universe of observing and acting.

2. Manage Conversations

Our traditional orientation toward communication is to focus on the content of a conversation. We learn to listen for the argument and the substance of what is being said, without simultaneously noticing that the conversation itself is always occurring against a background of shared meaning. For example, most companies note recurring problems between different groups. Thousands of hours are spent attempting to understand the content of each other's concerns and capabilities. If viewed as a conversation, the possibility of changing the relationship by changing the conversation becomes self-evident. If we are able to listen and speak from a different point of view, for example, where we might be aligned, we might discover that what had previously occurred as an argument now occurs as an expression of alignment with different pathways for action to choose from. We need to intentionally focus on the context of conversations as a way to solve problems and create breakthrough results. Specifically, in conversations we ask clients to continually ask themselves contextual questions such as: What are we committed to? What are our intentions? What are the concerns in the background that shape our conversations and actions?

Intentionally setting up and managing conversations helps to keep people focused, builds honesty and integrity, and enhances the team's ability to make better decisions more quickly.

3. Speak and Listen with Commitment

Language defines the human experience. More than anything else, it is language that distinguishes the human state from that of any other form of life on this planet. We are not simply purveyors and consumers of language, we *are* language. Most of us accept language as the air we breathe. It is invisible and exists all around us. We cannot get along without it, yet we take it for granted. Few people recognize the extent to which our thoughts, perceptions, and actions are shaped by language.

Most speaking doesn't move action or generate commitment. The majority of conversations we find ourselves in consist of expressing opinions, assessing people or situations, or asking questions. Once people see themselves and their organization as occurring in conversations, and realize the importance of managing the context of conversations, the next level of competency has to do with how to have effective conversations. For example, we distinguish five basic speech acts that constitute the actionable verbs by which human beings coordinate themselves. Remember, these are declarations, requests, promises, assessments, and assertions.[23]

Each of these speech acts has a distinctive role and implication in conversations for both the speaker and listener. A dec-

---

23   Searle, J. *The Re-discovery of the Mind.* Cambridge: MIT Press, 1992.

laration opens possibility, can complete something, can stop the action, and can even alter the common reality for everyone else. A simple example of a declaration is "I pronounce you man and wife." Requests and promises call for future action and bring forth some future state: "I request that you provide me feedback on my presentation by Thursday." Assessments provide an interpretation about the situation or circumstance as a foundation for mutual agreement and coordination, for example: "You are a collaborative manager." Assertions are statements of fact, something any set of observers would agree to be the case, for example: "The capital of France is Paris." The speaker commits, if asked, to be able to provide evidence for the truth of the statement.

Our speaking must be in concert with our listening. When the future condition being requested doesn't match that which is being promised, the result will be misunderstanding and lack of coordinated actions. When a declaration, for example, "I like it this way," is heard as an assessment ("I'm not willing to change") it will often give rise to an argument and invalidate what is being declared. Assertions may be true or false as a function of historical agreement, but in and of themselves are little more than "facts" without the power to guide action. Therefore, we need to keep checking in and asking questions to make sure what we are hearing is what people mean.

Most people don't have the distinction "listening." (Listening is to hear plus the interpretation of an observer, to hear is just biological.) It's true that people realize that they either are listening or they are not listening, but most people can't determine *how* they are listening. For example, in one company's product development team, a new person joined the group, and in her first meeting she presented an idea for a new product that she was excited about. One of the group members (we'll call him Bob) disagreed with her and they moved on. In subsequent meetings we began to notice that the new person would always disagree with Bob, regardless of the merits of his idea. After some coaching sessions with this individual, we realized that because Bob had been so quick to disagree with her during her first meeting, from then on she listened to Bob, not for what he had to say, but for what she could disagree with.

We often teach people that there are different ways to listen to one another, and like we set up different kinds of conversations, we also set up different ways to listen in conversations. Specifically we ask that people listen *for* certain things, depending on their agenda. For example, we may ask that people listen *for* possibility when they are stuck on a problem. We may also ask that people listen *for* alignment when they can't agree on a decision. There are many different things to listen *for* in conversations, and in mastering this competency we need to be responsible both for requesting how we want people to listen to us, and for noticing how we are listening to others. When a culture shifts from one based on prediction and control to one based on commitment and effective coordination, the competencies for listening and speaking in conversations become central.

When a culture shifts from one based on prediction and control to one based on commitment and effective coordination, the competencies for listening and speaking in conversations become central.

4. Make Assessments of Value

I have found that the most difficult of all of the aforementioned speech acts to master is that of assessment. This is, I believe, due to most people thinking that assessments are either true or false. This is a common problem in creative efforts, where people aren't able to prove a proposition but are nonetheless committed to it as a possibility. In most organizations, the lack of clear understanding that assessments are never true or false will lead to debates over which is true, when in fact neither can ever be "proved." Assessments can only be valid or invalid, grounded or ungrounded.

As a practical matter, making assessments of value is a primary component in most managerial and leadership roles, although not normally judged to be a competency per se. Rather, we relate to senior people as "knowing" the way things are and normally listen to their assessments as facts rather than as points of view.

5. Build Relationships Intentionally

We rarely consider relating to be a competency. In our conventional culture, a person who is good at relating is considered to be a "people person." He or she is thought to have the "right" types of personalities or sensibilities. We normally consider relationship to be a function of "chemistry" or perhaps "connection," but not something that is intentionally designed. Most of us recognize that when we go out of our way to know someone, more often than not something unexpected or positive will result. We find out that we have kids the same age, for example, or that we went to the same graduate school.

Building an intentional relationship requires that we believe and act as if we are fully responsible and accountable for the quality of a relationship. To consciously design relationships, we must engage in conversations that have to do with sharing our commitments, apologizing, asking for forgiveness, acknowledging the other person, and/or promising something of value to them. Building intentional relationships is about having each person get what they want and being able to feel fully self-expressed. It is not about manipulating people into getting them to do what *you* want them to do; rather it is about getting them to do what *they* want to do.

6. Acknowledge and Appreciate Each Other

This competency has to do with observing what is occurring for people and acknowledging what is so. If a person is performing well it is just as important to acknowledge that than it is to acknowledge his or her mistakes.

The purpose of candid and comprehensive acknowledgment is understanding, fulfillment, completion, and being fully self-expressed. Just as in any game, it is important that people be mentally and physically present. This cannot happen if people aren't acknowledged or are incomplete with some prior effort or work. Lack of completion leads to resentment and resignation. The competent leader in a rapidly changing environment needs to notice everything and acknowledge everyone for everything all the time. Doing this is natural when there is a genuine appreciation for people and their ambition. With appreciation comes compassion for what it takes to work in the face of constant uncertainty.

The purpose of candid and comprehensive acknowledgment is understanding, fulfillment, completion, and being fully self-expressed.

7. Declare and Resolve Breakdowns

One of the most important enabling competencies is that of a "breakdown." A breakdown is defined as anything a person says is impeding the action to fulfill their commitments. When declared, they serve to stop the action and call for conversations to coordinate different views, inquire into what may be missing or in the way, and create new possibilities or redirect action. Breakdowns are not problems insofar as they do not exist in the absence of a commitment. This is easily seen simply by revoking or changing the commitment behind the breakdown, and the breakdown disappears.

In teaching this competency, breakdowns are shown to be positive and necessary for accomplishing breakthroughs and taking unprecedented action. They are revealed and become obvious when people make big commitments to accomplish something beyond the predictable. When breakdowns are declared, the process for their resolution is conversations with involved parties to align on an interpretation of what is missing or what needs to be modified in order to move forward.

... breakdowns are shown to be positive and necessary for accomplishing breakthroughs and taking unprecedented action.

The key question is "what is missing?" rather than "what is wrong?" In the latter instance, we tend to become embroiled in a long or complex analysis of why something has occurred. If people have different assessments of a situation, they are encouraged to ground their assessments (clarify and provide support for their point of view) and choose an interpretation that offers the most result for resolution, rather than become fixated on having to come up with the "right" answer. In a transforming organization, the enabler is flexibility within one's commitment, rather than attachment to a result that is usually elusive anyway. Asking "what's missing?" will almost always point to something that has been assumed, but has neither been explicitly distinguished nor addressed.

8. Enroll Each Other in Greater Possibilities

Enrollment is a competency that is counterintuitive in most organizational cultures. It is counterintuitive because most cultures operate in the view that to gain support one must persuade, convince, inform, or "sell" another on the merits of some offer. Enrollment in our view is the result of "showing" people a larger possibility for themselves which relates to their deeper commitments and concerns and connecting them to what is being offered. People will usually enroll themselves when they receive an offer in this context. Enrollment as a competency involves listening deeply to what people really want and are committed to, which is often not obvious even to themselves. The orientation of a person who is enrolling is to serve and empower other people, not to get them to change their minds or agree with the offer.

Enrollment begins from an assumption that people are already committed to something that the offer will enable or support.

9. Coordinate Actions Effectively

From the perspective of viewing the organization as a network of relationships, effective coordination involves managing conversations and actions composed primarily of requests and promises. Business processes that lack clarity of this basic structure of human relationships will tend to lack flexibility when there are breakdowns. Attitudes of complacency, cynicism, resistance, or resignation will result. In the transformational approach, coordination takes into account and includes breakdowns in committed conversations.

effective in the domain of context which begins to change behavior is through teaching the enabling competencies. This will get the work required by the change effort to be done faster, better, and with more innovation.

CHAPTER 12

THE TRANSFORMATIONAL APPROACH

PRESENT AND EVALUATE THE CURRENT SITUATION OF THE BUSINESS

The case for change defines the urgency and magnitude of change required in an organization. Only once an organization has a clear and shared understanding about these dimensions and identifies where it is, vis-à-vis where it wants to be, can a transformational process be successful. The analytical framework and tools we use assess an organization's performance identify the critical outcomes and define key business drivers that will, in turn, inform the transformational process moving forward. The intention of this process is not to drown the company in analytics and data; rather, it is an opportunity to validate the passion and intuition of the company's leaders with the appropriate amount of analytic rigor.

Once the company has identified its case for change and has discussed in detail all of the elements listed above, we work with its members in identifying how their organizational behaviors have both affected and contributed to their current condition, as well as how they anticipate these behaviors will affect their condition moving forward. It is important to make the connection between the company's business agenda and their "culture" as a means to building a sustainable capability for change. To achieve a lasting transformation, a company must identify its persistent behavior patterns and intervene at the *source* of these behaviors. We call this source the *Operating State*. The Operating State is a set of unseen, implicit rules that shape the behavior of the organization and create unexamined boundaries for what can be done, said, or even thought. The term *Operating State* includes what most people describe as culture, but goes beyond it. We have given it this wording to demonstrate that it includes within it both the strategic and the structural approach. An organization's Operating State will determine its ability to adapt to change, both internal and external.

Diagnosis of the current Operating State is based on interviews and observations of the company both in cross-functional meetings and in daily work. The consultant looks for *recurring* complaints, breakdowns, dissatisfactions, issues, unfulfilled possibilities, and other sorts of interpreted explanations for not producing the results intended or required in their competitive reality. The point is to distinguish the relationship between explicit goals and objectives, and "the way it really is around here." One also needs to listen for the assessments that people have about the people as well as the related strategic and structural aspects of the organization. For example, someone might say, "We need better systems and processes for coordination." Often what people really mean when they say something like this is that the processes for coordination aren't working because there are no lines of clear accountability. Assessing the Operating State helps to find the gaps between what is being communicated and what is really happening.

We can distinguish four *core perspectives*, held both individually and collectively, that enable executives to unearth, examine, and shift the behaviors of the organization: power and limits: contention; identity; and learning (see Figure C). If we look at limits in a typical organization, what we will usually notice is that people don't feel empowered to make the choices they need to make. For example, in one company we worked with, the employees generally regarded the CEO as a domineering, old-line autocrat. Their Operating State was one of deep despair. They were truly resigned about the possibility of making anything new happen in their organization. Every time a new or innovative idea was surfaced, it was immediately shut down by others, based on their belief about not being able to get it past the CEO. In essence, their reactions perpetuated the organization's Operating State, creating a vicious circle from which they couldn't escape.

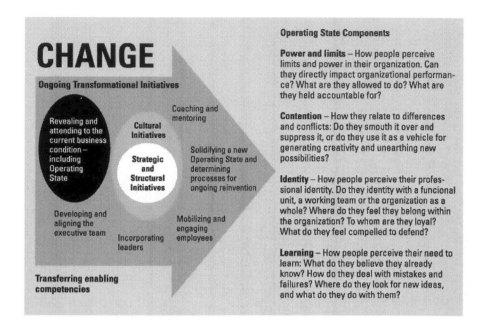

Figure C: Revealing and Attending to the Current Business Condition

In most organizations, *contentious* situations typically devolve into people thinking that they always have to be nice to one another, and thus important issues are often smoothed over or avoided. A middle manager in a service organization, for example, put it this way: "I would never bring up a problem with my boss because knowing him, he would take it personally, and I don't want to lose my job, or have him hate me."

In terms of *identity*, some companies are set up with functional identities; in others it is based on titles; and in still others, like retail, it is based on sales volume. When we determine where the employees' identity resides, we can often begin to shift it towards a more enterprise-wide sense of identity that allows for actions to be coordinated in a more focused way.

Finally, *learning* is a critical part of an organization's Operating State, and we are frequently challenged by a company's inability to learn for itself. As consultants, we often find that our clients use us to stop their own thinking, and we constantly have to be aware of this to make sure they are creating fresh ideas for themselves.

The paradox, posed by Einstein, is that "There are problems which simply cannot be solved thinking the way we thought when we created them." This is a particularly important assertion when working with engineers and other technical people who believe that the world is composed of problems and that their success is directly related to their skills as problem solvers. Revealing the current Operating State produces the conclusion that "we can't get there from here." This is a serious breakdown for the leadership, because they must confront that they are either misleading the organization with their corporate plans, or they need a breakthrough in their thinking and competencies to pull off their game.

*...everything we do to try to change the background condition will actually reinforce it. ...The only possibility is to create a **new** condition, which includes the current Operating State but isn't limited by it, and which provides for new possibilities and actions to appear.*

Specifically, it is critical to engage people in deeply examining and declaring what it is that they personally stand *for*, as the means for beginning to generate a new way of working together. The ambition of the leaders not only reflects a deep commitment to their values and the possibilities they see, but also simultaneously will produce a different *relationship* to their current state. The previously transparent now becomes observable, and therefore actionable to both the individual and the

171

group. Through time, the old Operating State begins to dissolve because it has less power over the participants, and a new Operating State emerges naturally, as an expression of authentic human concern and commitment.

DEVELOP AND ALIGN THE EXECUTIVE TEAM

The next phase pays close attention to bonding with and coaching the executive team. Executive team alignment entails partnering around desired culture, strategies, and business results. Authentic alignment is a process, not a one-time event. What passes for "alignment" is frequently, at best, agreement or compliance. One executive described it as "malicious obedience." The difference between alignment and agreement is that one can be aligned around a goal but have a different point of view about how to get there. The costs of "cosmetic" alignment are that it rapidly deteriorates, people compromise their true ambitions, and ultimately it produces disappointing results. Being aligned is not a willingness to "go along with"; rather, it is a commitment to work a new way.

We shouldn't underestimate the amount of energy required to gain alignment. Old habits die hard, especially with leaders. The reason they are leaders in the first place is that they have learned how to use the old system to get ahead. As such, they also have the most at risk, so we need to constantly make sure that they know what they want for themselves, each other, and their organizations. The real challenge is to get beyond the "whatever you say" mentality of executive decision-making and consensus. In each circumstance we need to ask the team, and ourselves "How do we create the environment of trust so that the question of authenticity isn't constantly undermining alignment?" Throughout this process we need keep checking to see if the executive members are being straight with one another.

LAUNCH STRATEGIC, STRUCTURAL, AND CULTURAL INITIATIVES

When the leadership of the enterprise is aligned around their vision, the key performance indicators, their performance targets, and their goals and objectives, many questions and opportunities will exist related to how work is accomplished and what the overall organizational design will look like. In most cases a company will undertake the creation of a business strategy based upon its view of the market, the competition, emerging technologies, and an assessment of its own strengths and weaknesses.

INTRODUCE STRATEGIC/STRUCTURAL AND CULTURAL INITIATIVES:

- Analyzing and documenting current practices and strategies.
- Designing the future state, which includes a reworking of current processes as well as creating new ones.
- Conducting a gap analysis by determining the differences between the current practices and culture and that of the desired state.
- Implementing a new operating design including training people in the new practices.

Within these elements are four distinct dimensions of the business that need to be addressed: the business process itself, roles and responsibilities, measurement criteria, and tools and techniques.

During this part of the transformational process we begin to implement some structural and procedural initiatives, as well as cultural ones. For example, we may launch a cross-functional HR redesign team and teach the members skills for resolving conflict.

INCORPORATE LEADERS

After the executive team is aligned around their vision and strategy and the various strategic/structural and cultural initiatives have been launched, we then need to work on incorporating the next level of leaders in the organization. Without their authentic buy-in and commitment, the organization will not be able to successfully implement the change program throughout the organization. "Leaders" can be defined in various ways, depending on the company's goals and objectives. For example, leaders can be defined as managers in business units, vice presidents of departments, or "change agents" across different levels and functional accountabilities in the company. Most often we focus on the level of management just below the senior team, anywhere from fifty to five hundred people, depending on the size of the corporation.

Incorporation is the process of merging individual points of view into a shared vision that leads to building authentic ownership of a new future for the company. When it is successful, the relationship between senior and middle managers is transformed. Initiative displaces asking for permission, candor displaces guarded communication, and accountability displaces excuses. The process is much the same as aligning the executive team, but it is important to note, however, that this is not a process of reporting what the executive team has decided and asking for agreement.

Authentic buy-in occurs only when someone has ample opportunity to engage and challenge a decision and make an informed choice. This process is most powerful when the executive team engages the participants from a clean slate. In other words, rather than presenting their findings, the leadership team starts with a blank page to discover what aspirations already exist. The executives' perspectives on performance levels should be equally weighted with that of all other participants. Experience shows that, in most cases, the collective ambition of this group is *higher* than that of the executive team.

*Experience shows that, in most cases, the collective ambition of this group or new participants is **higher** than that of the executive team.*

Incorporating this next level of leadership is critical to the organization's success in implementing and sustaining a change program, as they will have to be the champions of the program for their staff. Many executives have bypassed this group altogether, as they are often old-time employees who have worked their way up the ranks and are often resistant to these types of "interruptive" efforts. Failure to incorporate this group will often create a self-fulfilling prophecy of resistance and cynicism. Their involvement in the change process will have a profound impact either positively or negatively on what the change program can ultimately accomplish. To realize a positive outcome, these leaders will have to commit to unprecedented straight talk, shift their leadership style from that of manager to that of coach, and deal with breakdowns in a way that creates opportunity. This change in style often entails a lot of patience, persistence, and hard work.

Like the executive team, this group works to develop a deep understanding (and owning) of the current business situation, the desired future, and the internal conditions that will be needed for success. The members don't necessarily create a road map of how to get from Point A to Point B in the initial phases; we usually just try to get them to align around the Kips, the performance targets, and the critical next steps. This process can't be accomplished alone, or in a single meeting; it is much more of a journey than an event. For example, one company thought it had succeeded in incorporating the top fifty-five managers. Subsequently, it sent ten of the participants into a separate set of meetings to develop a plan for engaging the rest of the organization. When the subset returned, the energy of the larger group had dissipated, and they viewed the smaller group as unrealistic and naive. It took several weeks to get the whole group realigned. What they realized was that they needed to have all fifty-five managers involved in ironing out an approach for engaging the rest of the organization, and each of them would need to be intimately involved in, and accountable for, the roll-out of this process.[24]

A critical barrier to get over during this stage is shifting from a command-and-control style of leading to one that enables and empowers. By showing their willingness to share ownership for decisions, top executives relinquish absolute control, and managers at the next level realize that they are critically involved in creating the future, not just following dictates. This is a contagious condition and will almost always be emulated by the next level of leaders. For some, giving up absolute control feels like abdicating their responsibility to lead. Many managers during this process need to be taught how to lead from a different place (as a coach) in order to have the initiative be successful.

---

24   Gilbert, J. and B. Larson. "Mobilizing the Work Force for Results," *CSC Insights,* 1996.

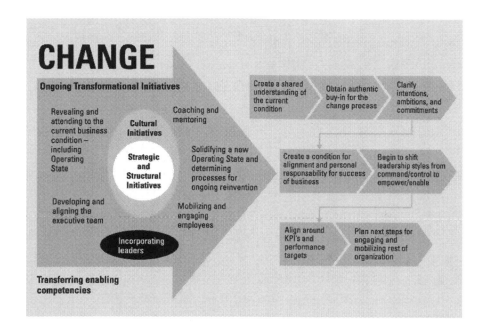

Figure D: Leadership Incorporation—A Process Overview

MOBILIZE AND ENGAGE THE ORGANIZATION

Sherlock Holmes once said, "The obvious is a very telling clue." Not only are we seeing books on organizations as ecological systems and networks of relationships,[25] but we are also seeing more and more experts arguing for engaging the masses as leaders in organizational change. Topics like coaching, loyalty, the importance of an organizational "soul," and "predictable miracles" have been proliferating the business best-seller list. We believe this movement is largely in response to the criticisms of the early strategic and structural approaches that engineered people right out of the change process. Our transformational approach strives to align and include *all* employees in the change process and mobilizes the entire organization around new visions and goals.

---

25   Bohm, D. and M. Edwards. *Changing Consciousness*. San Francisco: Harper, 1991. Wheatley, M. and Kellner-Rogers. *A Simpler Way*. San Francisco: Berrett-Koehler, 1996.

A manager must consider the possibility that employees don't resist change simply because they don't like change, but because they are resigned about their ability to make a difference. This resignation is frequently manifested as cynicism and resistance. To counter the cynicism, employees must be re-enrolled and challenged to take active roles in the future of their business. Mere understanding of the case for change and the company's vision is insufficient. Mobilization processes must be designed to rapidly engage people in personalizing the vision and initiating relevant local action in support of it (see Figure E). Mobilization is about "recapturing people's hearts," going well beyond understanding and agreement. The challenge includes reestablishing or expanding the credibility of senior managers while engaging all employees in the management of the business.

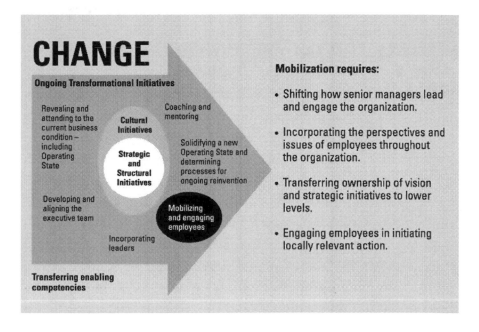

Figure E: Mobilize and Engage the Organization

The transformational approach maintains that "unleashing the human spirit" in the workplace is the key to a successful mobilization effort. "Spirit" is not used here to connote a metaphysical abstraction; rather it refers to a condition of full self-expression. Being fully self-expressed is at the heart of authenticity, relationship, and accomplishment. When people are fully expressed, related to, and honest with one another, they are able to produce results that far exceed their expectations. People want to be themselves whether it is at home, at work, or at play. They are seeking this consistency in their lives and desperately want to put away the masks that represent their interpretations of what it will take to be liked and accepted.

Unleashing the human spirit of individuals in organizations entails recognizing these masks and knowing when we put them on. We have to be aware of, and accept, how we *are* before we can make choices about being a different way. This approach allows individuals and organizations to recognize and honor these masks by disclosing them and creating a safe space in which to be fully self-expressed. It is when all employees are truly striving to be whole and laughing at their own shortcomings that transformation can take place.

Engaging and mobilizing large numbers of people in the service of a common vision is not only a process of communication, but also of building relationships anew since, in most organizations, there may be a history of distrust, resentment, and resignation. The consultant must be able to distinguish these limiting background conversations as they manifest in moods and actions. This can be accomplished by creating opportunities for employees who have been introduced to the basic distinctions of the enabling competencies to dialogue with each other. To create change, we claim that all people need is a chance to be heard in a safe environment and have permission to express all of the background noise that shapes and influences their perceptions and behaviors.

True employee engagement requires that everyone recognize that creating a new culture is continuous and will be uncomfortable insofar as the process reveals that which has been avoided or covered up. Human beings will always forget and get sucked into old habits. It is important to present the process without creating the expectation that it will be easy. A bold person cannot avoid risks. When circumstances change, there are sometimes other responsible actions that need to be communicated appropriate to restore relationships, build new competencies, or change course altogether. The engagement process emphasizes that there are particular conversations and practices that are necessary to master if we are to build an organizational culture based on commitment rather than on prediction. Among these, for example, are conversations and practices in which acknowledgment, letting go, and asking for and giving forgiveness become explicit and necessary.

True employee engagement requires that everyone recognize that creating a new culture is continuous and will be uncomfortable insofar as the process reveals that which has been avoided or covered up.

Practically speaking, the whole organization is mobilized for change through specific incidents and activities. Often in this phase, reinvention action teams are set up to help redesign the core business processes, develop new businesses, or explore joint ventures. Throughout this phase, specific incidents are created and used to reveal, challenge, and interrupt the Operating State and begin to shift it. We call these incidents "defining moments," events that are sufficiently disruptive to provide an opportunity for radical change. A defining moment can occur spontaneously, or it can be a deliberate and conscious action to reveal and shift the Operating State of the organization.

SOLIDIFY A NEW OPERATING STATE AND DETERMINE PROCESSES FOR ONGOING REINVENTION

Awareness of Operating States creates an ongoing opportunity to reveal and shift how employees are "being" in the face of competitive demands. In this phase the consultant would assist the corporation in developing teams and processes geared to ongoing business reinvention. This is largely done through practicing a set of *cultural disciplines* (see Figure F). By disciplines we mean rigorous, practiced forms of behavior each individual in the organization begins to develop and master.

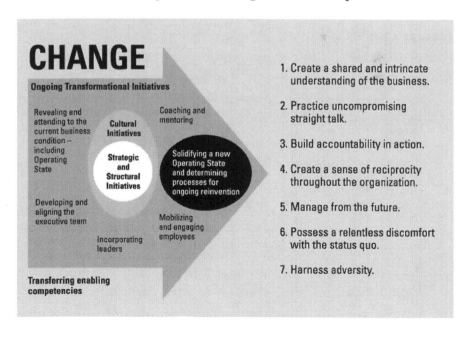

Figure F: Solidifying a New Operating State—Practicing Cultural Disciplines

SEVEN DISCIPLINES

The seven disciplines that an organization needs to practice in order to sustain a new operating state are:

1. Create a shared and intricate understanding of the business by opening experiential and continual channels for learning, as opposed to traditional one-way communication.

2. Use straight talk as a way to surface contention in order to generate creativity and build trust, rather than as a means to manipulate or dominate.

3. Generate "accountability in action" to encourage people to be responsible for the business as a whole and help each other solve problems, rather than operating from denial, blame, and internal competition.

4. Build reciprocity throughout the organization as a way to incorporate people in acting as stakeholders for the company, while at the same time, giving them something back (rewards and/or acknowledgments) they can be proud of.

5. Manage from the future rather than from what people already know to be true in the past.

6. Ask people to have a **relentless discomfort with the status quo**, meaning to guard against complacency and always challenging people to be the best they can be.

7. Harness adversity in a way that builds creativity and openness rather than creates an environment of distrust and resentment.

What constitutes a discipline? At one level, it is an enduring pattern of social behavior that includes unconscious patterns and habits. Habits typically are automatic behaviors that are not consciously chosen. Disciplines, on the other hand, are chosen and executed consciously. In other words, habits are

182

mindless and disciplines are mindful. An organization needs to build and mold each discipline simultaneously, though at times each will have a different level of priority. In addition, we have found that disciplines are largely emergent phenomena. That is, once people begin to practice one they can't help but to begin practice the others.

By practicing these disciplines, a company will be able to sustain a new Operating State and begin to develop some ongoing processes for reinvention. Again, it is important to note that the organization's Operating State is not static. The company will need to continually design and refine its Operating State and intentionally focus on the four core perspectives that give it access to seeing where it is presenting vs. where it needs to be.

TRANSFER COACHING CAPABILITIES

As a new Operating State based on commitment emerges and people begin to relate to the future as a possibility, new styles of working become inevitable. Throughout the transformational process, consultants act as coaches to people at every level to build these basic competencies. When someone is working on a problem, coaching entails engaging that person to figure the answer out for him- or herself. For example, when building this competency we often ask that the employees get in pairs to discuss an issue that is particularly difficult or one where they feel stuck. We ask the person serving as the coach to work with the other person to help them resolve the problem, following simple guidelines: no giving advice and no commiserating. This is difficult for most people, particularly for people who are experts in certain areas, and would normally want to provide their colleagues with the answers. This is not to say never give advice or commiserate; rather it seems to point out that the person being coached most often already has the answers, and just needs to be asked the right questions.

Coaches are people that are committed to someone else's commitments. They provide an objective eye and can see what the employee can't or won't see. Their intention is to help employees realize their goals and objectives. The result of successful coaching is self-generated action in the direction of a goal or commitment. Effective coaching is not based in knowledge, but is *based in vision*, where one is looking from and what another is looking toward.

Coaching requires a relationship that grants permission to be coached. Without permission, whatever takes place is not coaching but rather directing or controlling. Coaches focus on what is missing, not what is wrong (like a critic does). A coach's role is not to provide the answers, but to provide access to new possibilities and more effective action by helping others to think differently about the issues facing them. Finally, for coaching to be effective there must be a connection between the mentoring and demonstrable results consistent with the commitment of the person being coached.

A coach's role is not to provide the answers, but to provide access to new possibilities and more effective action by helping others to think differently about the issues facing them.

The primary new competencies that are developed through coaching are listening, observing conversations, relating, enrolling, resolving breakdowns, managing from the future, and generating alignment. We propose that an organization adopt coaching as the primary context for managing the organization because when mastered, it provides a framework for focusing on working with people and their commitments.

Coaching in an organization provides an environment in which both managers and those they are managing have equal value in the game and are learning from each other while maintaining different roles and competencies.

BUSINESS RESULTS AND OUTCOMES

What are the tactical benefits of using the transformational approach as the basis for an organization's large-scale change initiative? Broadly stated, the behavioral results are empowerment, possibility, inquiry and alignment. This are absolutely critical for a company's change initiative to have the momentum and commitment required to be successful. Empowered people make better decisions and take accountability for their areas of responsibility and for the company as a whole. Finally, alignment facilitates the process of constantly changing our objectives and outcomes to meet changing demands in the marketplace.

Companies utilizing this approach are reaping unprecedented results. For example, in one manufacturing company:

- Engineering change requests and order backlogs each decreased by approximately 70%.
- Purchase parts shortages decreased by 93%.
- Manufacturing parts shortages decreased by 90%.
- Quality effectiveness almost doubled that of the original goal.

IN ANOTHER ORGANIZATION, TEAMS FOCUSING ON NEW PRODUCT DEVELOPMENT:

- Cut the time to market in half.
- Leaped ahead of the competition in performance capabilities.

- Invented ways to have existing technology far outperform what was previously thought possible.

IN YET ANOTHER COMPANY:

- Employee teams were able to reduce their costs of a major development project by over $13 million.
- A regional sales office that had consistently been at the bottom half of producers in their company outperformed all other regions in the country.
- A $40-million projected loss that year produced instead a $5-million profit.

In short, speed flattens the competition. Those who take hold of these new ways of thinking and acting in their work environments will have a competitive edge in the future.

CONCLUSION

The transformational approach to change management allows a company to get at what is beneath all the things that are in its way of becoming a world-class organization. It goes beyond putting a Band-Aid on a wound and allows the organization to sustainably heal what ails it. The ontological underpinnings of this work allow an organization to experience itself and its world more directly. An environment is created where the context is just as important as the content and becomes the main lever for creating sustainable change. In essence, this is accomplished by getting all the background conversations on the table and allowing people to create their present situations moment by moment, without all of the "baggage" that usually holds people up. By having the team members unearth and share their commitments, they can more easily move through contentious situations and solve difficult problems.

The nine enabling competencies are, in essence, the practices that allow a person to be effective in the domain of context. Teaching an organization's members about these competencies and having people reach mastery in each area has greatly transformed the nature of the organizations with which we have worked. Finally, the seven-step transformational process represents a holistic offering of the content and processes that need to be put in place in order to manage from a contextual point of view. In sum, the transformational approach will allow an organization to not only keep up with but lead and prosper in the next millennium.

BIOGRAPHY

JAMES C. SELMAN is a recognized leader and authority in the field of organizational transformation and culture change. For over thirty-five years Jim has been helping leaders and companies achieve breakthroughs in their performance. He was the first to practice entrepreneur leadership within private and public organizations, and for more than twenty years he has been devoted to the development of leadership in ontological design to identify the need for manifesting organizational change, distinguishing the leverage points for leaders and managers to generate change and develop a new technology for accelerating the pace for transformation.

Today, he consults regularly in English, French, and Spanish to organizations and governments in Europe, Mexico, and North and South America as CEO of *ParaComm Partners International*, since 2002 in partnership with *Merkaba Partners Consulting*. He is principal contributor to the *Serene Ambition* blog, *The Eldering Institute*, and since 2009 collaborates with the *Huffington Post*. He has been instrumental in building new theory and practical technologies in the field of management (including the concepts of "organizational transformation," "coaching," "the Merlin method for designing and the future," "breakthroughs," and "breakdowns") and in introducing new approaches to producing broad paradigm shifts. He has helped numerous multinational corporations and Fortune 500 companies (as well as the White House, Congress, and the US Air Force) mobilize people and build competencies in executive leadership, communication, relationship, business process design, and coordination. Jim was privileged to work in education and research with some of the leading thinkers and practitioners in the fields of transformation and management, including Dr. Fernando Flores, Warren Bennis, Peter Senge, Richard Pascal, Werner Erhard, and Ken Blanchard, among others.

As co-founder and CEO of Transformational Technologies, he influenced the development of more than two thousand American, European, and Latin American companies. He is a former member of the California Commission on Aging, a past director of the Breakthrough Foundation, a founder of Growing Older (a nonprofit for seniors' education) and a founding member of the Legacy XXI Institute.

In 2002 in Buenos Aires he gave together with *Merkaba Partners Consulting* an international seminar entitled "Crisis or Possibility," open to the Argentine community, on creative practices for the development of new capabilities to create new futures in a context of fast and uncertain changes.

In 2006, he was involved in a groundbreaking coaching conference in Vancouver, British Columbia. Forty-three key thought leaders from fourteen nations gathered to discuss the current challenges facing the coaching industry and to invent new possibilities for moving the profession forward. In early 2008, Jim participated with twenty-two other transformational leaders and officials in the United Nations to begin a dialogue to distinguish the emerging paradigm and how transformational leadership principles might offer a breakthrough in empowering developing nations and assisting leaders in those countries to undertake full-spectrum responses to their most pressing issues and intractable problems.

Some of Jim's accomplishments in working with both public and private sector clients include:

- Design and leadership of National Program Initiatives of the United States in the areas of environmental protection, drug and alcohol abuse, and economic development on behalf of various government agencies, including the White House and the United States Congress (1980).
- Development of Strategies for Corporate Reinvention— transformation—including the design of original approaches to building leadership competencies in the telecommunications, financial, food, health, aerospace, oil, and electrical utility industries.
- Design and implementation of new paradigms and research related to human and cultural aspects of the emerging paradigms and great acquisitions. A landmark example involved a five-billion-dollar acquisition affecting four thousand employees that was completed to the satisfaction of the people from both organizations in less than six months.
- Work with well-known scholars and leaders of organizations showing the new theory of language as an emerging management paradigm, and in the development of many concepts and essential principles that rule organizational performance.
- Development of a leadership course "Coaching for Breakthroughs, Commitment and Change," seen as a component in all overall strategy to transform the culture of the

Canadian government to become a more citizen-focused and effective learning organization.

- Work with many of the major federal departments of the Canadian government in the design and implementation of transformational strategies.
- A BA degree with majors in social psychology and philosophy.

Currently he is guest professor to the Leadership Program of the *Instituto de Desarrollo Directivo Integral (IDDI)*, Francisco de Vitoria University, Madrid, Spain. In the past five years, Jim has come to appreciate that age is one of the most fundamental factors affecting how we experience our day to day lives, the possibilities we have and how we relate to ourselves and other people. He is founder of the *The Eldering Institute* and author of the book *The Elder* with Dr Mark Cooper.

BIBLIOGRAPHY

Bateson, G. *Steps to an Ecology of Mind.* New York: Ballantine Books, 1972.

Beer, M. and E. Walton. "Developing the Competitive Organization; Interventions and Strategies." American Psychologist, 1990, 45.

Bohm, D. and M. Edwards. *Changing Consciousness.* San Francisco: Harper, 1991.

Bolman, L.G. and T.E. Deal. *Reframing Organizations.* San Francisco: Jossey- Bass, 1991.

Carr, C. *Choice, Chance & Organizational Change.* New York: AMACOM, 1996.

Champy, J. *Reengineering Management.* New York: Harper Business, 1995.   Fishman, C. "The 10 Laws of Change That Never Change." Fast Company

Magazine, 1997 (8).

Fritz, R. *Corporate Tides.* San Francisco: Berrett-Koehler, 1996.

Gilbert, J. and B. Larson. "Mobilizing the Work Force for Results." CSC Insights, 1996.

Goldman, S.L., Nagel, R.N., and K. Preiss. *Agile Competitors and Virtual Organizations.* New York: Van Nostrand Reinhold, 1995.

Gouillart, F. and Kelly, J. *Transforming the Organization.* New York: McGraw- Hill, 1995.

Handy, C. *Beyond Uncertainty.* Boston, MA: HES Press, 1996.

Hargrove, R. *Masterfull Coaching.* San Francisco: Jossey-Bass, 1995.

Hawken, P. *The Ecology of Commerce.* New York: Harper Collins, 1993.

Heidegger, M. *Being and Time.* Translated by J. Macquarte and E. Robinson. New York: Harper & Row, 1968.

Helgeson, S. *The Web of Inclusion.* New York: Currency/ Doubleday, 1995.

Jaworski, J. *Synchronicity: The Inner Path of Leadership.* San Francisco: Berrett-Koehler Publishers, 1996.

Mohrmann, S.A., Cohen, S.G. and A.M. Mohrmann, Jr. *Designing Team Based Organizations.* San Francisco: Jossey Bass, 1995.

Moore, J. "Predators and Prey; A New Ecology of Competition," *Harvard Business Review,* May–June 1993.

Oppenheimer, P. and E. Zalta. "On the Logic of the Ontological Argument" in J. Tomberlin (ed.) *Philosophical Perspectives* 5: Ridgeview (1991): 509-29. (Publicación recomendada para obtener más información sobre ontología.)

Oshry, B. *The Possibilities of Organization.* Boston: Power & Systems, Inc., 1986.

Reichheld, F. *The Loyalty Effect: The Hidden Force Behind Growth, Profits, and Lasting Value.* Cambridge; Harvard Business School Press, 1996.

Rosen, C. and M. Quarrey. "How Well Is Employee Ownership Working?" *Harvard Business Review*, September 1987.

Rosen, J. "The CEO Playbook—Detailed Description," N.° 00389-JIR-CEOPlay3- 10/96ems/cam; CSC Index confidential, 1996.

Searle, J. *The Re-discovery of the Mind.* Cambridge: MIT Press, 1992.

Stacey, R. *Complexity and Creativity in Organizations.* San Francisco: Berrett-Koehler, 1996.

Waldrop, M. *The Emerging Science at the Edge of Order and Chaos.* New York: Touchstone, 1992,

Wheatley, M. and Kellner-Rogers. *A Simpler Way.* San Francisco: Berrett-Koehler, 1996.

Whyte, D. *The Heart Aroused.* New York: Doubleday, 1994.

Winograd, T. and F. Flores. *Understanding Computers and Cognition: A New Foundation for Design.* Reading, MA: Addison-Wesley, 1987.